Aeschylus
Agamemnon

Aeschylus
Agamemnon

A new translation and
commentary by Philip de May

Introduction to the Greek Theatre
by P.E. Easterling

Series Editors: John Harrison and Judith Affleck

CAMBRIDGE
UNIVERSITY PRESS

CAMBRIDGE
UNIVERSITY PRESS

University Printing House, Cambridge CB2 8BS, United Kingdom

Cambridge University Press is part of the University of Cambridge.

It furthers the University's mission by disseminating knowledge in the pursuit of education, learning and research at the highest international levels of excellence.

www.cambridge.org
Information on this title: www.cambridge.org/9780521010757

© Cambridge University Press 2003

First published 2003
10th printing 2014

A catalogue record for this publication is available from the British Library

ISBN 978-0-521-01075-7 Paperback

ACKNOWLEDGEMENTS
Thanks are due to the following for permission to reproduce photographs:
pp. 1, 7, 46, 75, 110, Donald Cooper/Photostage; p. 25, © Copyright The British Museum; pp. 71, 83, Nobby Clark; p. 112, Ivan Kyncl.

Every effort has been made to reach copyright holders. The publishers would be glad to hear from anyone whose rights they have unknowingly infringed.

Map on p. x by Helen Humphreys.

Cover picture: *Clytaemnestra* by Baron Pierre-Narcisse Guérin, © Photo RMN/Ojeda – El Majd.

PERFORMANCE
For permission to give a public performance of this translation of *Agamemnon* please write to Permissions Department, Cambridge University Press, University Printing House, Shaftesbury Road, Cambridge CB2 8BS.

Contents

Preface

The aim of the series is to enable students to approach Classical plays with confidence and understanding: to discover the play within the text.

The translations are new. Many recent versions of Greek tragedy have been produced by poets and playwrights who do not work from the original Greek. The translators of this series aim to bring readers, actors and directors as close as possible to the playwrights' actual words and intentions: to create translations which are faithful to the original in content and tone; and which are speakable, with all the immediacy of modern English.

The notes are designed for students of Classical Civilisation and Drama, and indeed anyone who is interested in theatre. They address points which present difficulty to the reader of today: chiefly relating to the Greeks' religious and moral attitudes, their social and political life, and mythology.

Our hope is that students should discover the play for themselves. The conventions of the Classical theatre are discussed, but there is no thought of recommending 'authentic' performances. Different groups will find different ways of responding to each play. The best way of bringing alive an ancient play, as any other, is to explore the text practically, to stimulate thought about ways of staging the plays today. Stage directions in the text are minimal, and the notes are not prescriptive; rather, they contain questions and exercises which explore the dramatic qualities of the text. Bullet points introduce suggestions for discussion and analysis; open bullet points focus on more practical exercises.

If the series encourages students to attempt a staged production, so much the better. But the primary aim is understanding and enjoyment.

This translation of *Agamemnon* is based on the Greek text edited by Denys Page for Oxford University Press.

John Harrison
Judith Affleck

Background to the story of Agamemnon

(*The names of characters who appear in this play are printed in* **bold**.)

Agamemnon is the story of what happened to **Agamemnon** when he returned home to Argos at the end of the Trojan War. It assumes a familiarity with the history of Agamemnon's family, and with the events of the Trojan War and its aftermath.

Atreus was king of Argos. Atreus' brother Thyestes had an affair with Atreus' wife and hoped to become king himself. Atreus discovered this and banished Thyestes from Argos. He later pretended to relent and allowed Thyestes to return; however, he had Thyestes' children murdered (only one of Thyestes' sons – **Aegisthus** – escaped this fate), dismembered and served up at the banquet welcoming Thyestes back. Thyestes took a taste but then realised what he had done, vomited up what he had eaten and cursed Atreus and his descendants. According to some versions, this 'curse' was one of a series of evils afflicting the house of Atreus, going back to Tantalus (see *Genealogical table*, page ix).

Atreus had two sons: Agamemnon and Menelaus. Agamemnon inherited the throne and married **Clytaemnestra**; Menelaus married her sister Helen, nominally the daughter of the king of Sparta (but in fact daughter of Zeus), and thus himself became king of Sparta in due course. Later, however, Paris, a prince from Troy, while staying with Menelaus, abducted Helen and sailed back with her to Troy. Menelaus asked his elder brother Agamemnon to bring her back from Troy by force. Agamemnon gathered a large army with many heroes at the port of Aulis, but they were unable to sail across to Troy – the winds were blowing in the opposite direction, since the goddess Artemis was angry. Agamemnon sacrificed his daughter Iphigeneia to appease Artemis and favourable winds ensued. The expedition then sailed for Troy and fought the Trojans (under King Priam) for ten years. Many famous Greek and Trojan warriors were killed, but Troy was finally defeated by the trick of the Wooden Horse.

There are three main accounts of Agamemnon's homecoming in Homer's great poem the *Odyssey*. Nestor, who fought at Troy with Agamemnon, tells Odysseus' son (*Odyssey iii*, trans. Rieu):

> While we who were besieging Troy toiled at heroic tasks,
> Aegisthus spent his leisured days right in the heart of Argos
> where the horses graze, busy charming Agamemnon's wife

with his seductive talk. At first Queen Clytaemnestra turned a deaf ear to his dishonourable schemes. But when the fatal day came, appointed by the gods for her to yield, Aegisthus ... carried Clytaemnestra off to his own house, fond lover, willing lady.

Menelaus later tells Odysseus' son (*Odyssey iv*):

The warm tears rolled down Agamemnon's cheeks, he was so glad to see his country again. But his arrival was observed by a spy in a watch-tower, whom the cunning Aegisthus had posted there ... This man had been on the lookout in case the King should land unannounced ... Then Aegisthus devised a clever trap ... Agamemnon, never guessing that he was going to his doom, came up with him from the coast, and Aegisthus feasted him, then killed him as a man might fell an ox at its manger.

Odysseus visits the Underworld to obtain information to help him return home. While there, he meets the ghost of the dead Agamemnon, who tells him (*Odyssey xi*):

It was Aegisthus who plotted my destruction and with my accursed wife put me to death. He invited me to the palace, he feasted me, and he killed me as a man fells an ox at its manger. That was my most pitiful end. And all round me my companions were cut down in ruthless succession, like white-tusked swine slaughtered in the mansion of some rich and powerful lord, for a wedding, or a banquet, or a sumptuous private feast ... Yet the most pitiable thing of all was the cry I heard from **Cassandra**, daughter of Priam, whom that treacherous schemer Clytaemnestra murdered at my side. I raised my hands, but then beat them on the ground, dying, thrust through by a sword. The bitch turned her face aside, and could not even bring herself, though I was on my way to Hades, to shut my eyes with her hands or to close my mouth. There is nothing more degraded or shameful than a woman who can contemplate and carry out deeds like the hideous crime of murdering the husband of her youth. I had certainly expected a joyful welcome from my children and my servants when I reached my home. But now, in the depths of her villainy, she has branded with infamy not herself alone but the whole of her sex, even the virtuous ones, for all time to come.

Later authors often adapted these stories or diverged from them. Aeschylus accepts that Agamemnon dies on his return from Troy, but the details and the cause are open for Aeschylus to decide. In Aeschylus' version, for example, the guard in the watch-tower is set not by Aegisthus, as in *Odyssey iv*, but by Agamemnon's wife, Clytaemnestra. Aeschylus, Sophocles and Euripides, the three tragedians whose works are extant, all wrote plays connected with the legend of Agamemnon's death (Sophocles' *Electra*, Euripides' *Electra* and *Orestes*) which have survived, and each playwright gives the story a different slant.

Agamemnon is the first play of a trilogy known as the *Oresteia*: the only complete ancient Greek trilogy to have survived. In the second play, the *Choephoroi* (*Libation Bearers*), Agamemnon's son Orestes returns and kills his mother Clytaemnestra to avenge his father. In the third play, the *Eumenides* (*Kindly Ones*), a court is established to judge Orestes for his matricide.

Genealogical table

Genealogy of the house of Tantalus (also known as the house of Pelops/Atreus).

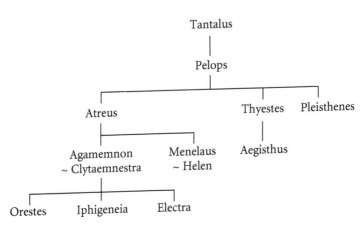

Map of Ancient Greece

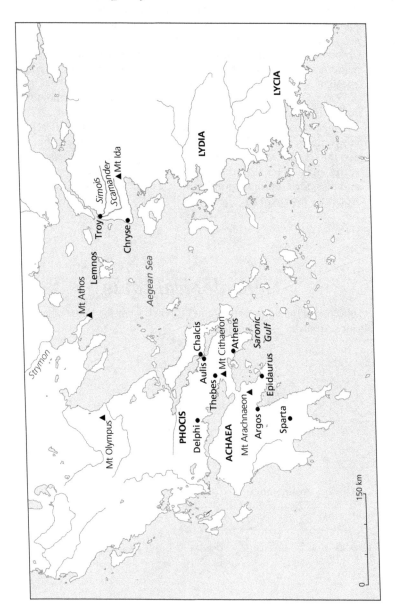

List of characters

WATCHMAN   servant of the palace at Argos

CHORUS   old men of Argos

CLYTAEMNESTRA   queen of Argos, wife of King Agamemnon

HERALD   messenger from the army at Troy

AGAMEMNON   king of Argos and commander of the
expedition against Troy

CASSANDRA   daughter of Priam, king of Troy, and
Agamemnon's prize of war

AEGISTHUS   cousin to King Agamemnon

*Agamemnon, from the
National Theatre
production, London, 1981.*

PROLOGUE (1–39)

The prologue is the part of a tragedy before the entry of the chorus (see **The Chorus** page 4); often a character sets the scene for the audience, who do not necessarily know the play's setting. This play takes place in front of King Agamemnon's palace in Argos; it opens with a speech by a watchman, probably crouching on the palace roof. Since Greek tragedies were performed in daylight, the impression of night is created by the watchman's words. The image of the fire and a lonely beacon with which the trilogy opens (see *Background to the story*) recurs with the procession of massed torches at its close.

1 an end to this work   The work of the watchman is to stay awake all night and watch for a signal of fire (9–10) that Troy, which has now been under siege by the Greeks for ten years, has been captured.

The sons of Atreus

3 Atreidae   A plural word, meaning the two sons of Atreus: Agamemnon, king of Argos, and Menelaus, king of Sparta. Greek heroes are commonly referred to by their patronymic (father's name). Here, as several times in the play, the plural is used to refer to one brother only (see note on 384, line 511).

8 signal from a fire-beacon   A series of beacons has been stationed between Troy and Argos and will be lit in sequence to relay news of Troy's capture as quickly as possible; later there is a lengthy description of how the relay works (267–302).

Male and female

10–11 the authority of/A woman's mind   The woman is Clytaemnestra, Agamemnon's wife: she has authority (see **Authority** page 26) in Argos in her husband's absence. For a woman in ancient Greece to hold any sort of authority was highly irregular (see below) and here is occasioned by Agamemnon's absence. This first mention of Clytaemnestra establishes that though she is a woman, she has qualities that the watchman would expect to find in a man (see **Male and female** pages 30 and 48, line 1597).

The house

18 this house   The ancient Greeks often use house (*oikos, domos*) to mean the people inside rather than the building itself; thus 'the house' may signify not the actual palace but the family, past and present, and slaves who live in it. Usually the male head (*kurios*) of the household presides over the house.

WATCHMAN I beg the gods for an end to this work,
To my year-long vigil. Lying
High up on the roof of the Atreidae like a watchdog,
I have come to know the throng of nightly stars,
Those that bring summer and winter to mankind,   5
Lords of light, stars bright in the sky –
When they set and when they rise. And all the while
I am on my guard for the signal from a fire-beacon,
Which will bring a blazing message of flame from Troy –
News of its capture; such is the authority of   10
A woman's mind: expectant, determined like a man's.
My bed, often shifted during the night,
Is unvisited by dreams and now sodden with dew,
Since fear – not sleep – stands over it,
So my eyes never firmly close in sleep.   15
Whenever I want to sing or hum,
To shape some soothing song as an antidote to sleep,
I weep for this house and grieve for its difficulties:
It is not managed as well as it once was.
But now I wish that the fire of good news would appear   20
Through the darkness and put a welcome end to my work.

22 Hail The long-awaited beacon is sighted.

28 cry of joyous welcome This loud cry (*ololugmos*) is one of joy, usually associated with women, and used to honour the gods (568, 576, 1207) or thank them.

29 Ilium is an alternative name for Troy – hence the *Iliad*, Homer's epic poem set at Troy.

33 thrown me this triple six The watchman uses an image from a game. Looking out for the beacon fire has in the end produced the best possible result for him: in gaming language, he has thrown a triple six, the highest throw. Agamemnon too has had his own 'lucky throw': he has captured Troy.

36–7 A great ox/Stands on my tongue The watchman uses a colloquial metaphor to mean that he will not speak about other goings-on in the palace.

The watchman's speech (1–39)
- What do we learn about the character and attitudes of the watchman?
- Does he give any clues that all is not well in the house of Atreus? What notes of foreboding can be found in his speech?
- How does the watchman communicate the loneliness and length of his watch?

PARODOS (ENTRY OF THE CHORUS) (40–243)
At this point in the original performance, the Chorus would have entered through the side entrances (*parodoi*) to arrive at the *orchēstra*, the circular dance-floor in front of the stage (see *Introduction to the Greek Theatre*). The *parodos* is both the Chorus' entrance and their first song: in this translation choral passages are centred. This *parodos* is the longest in extant tragedy; its subject-matter can be divided into four sections: 40–103, 104–48, 149–69, 170–243.

The Chorus
A chorus in Greek tragedy is a group of 12 to 15 unnamed characters who sing and dance together between scenes or *episodes*. Once they enter, they are present for the rest of the play. They express their thoughts on what is currently happening, or they may relate other events which are of relevance to the action. Sometimes they speak during the action itself but they only rarely participate in it (see **The Chorus debate** page 100).

The Chorus in *Agamemnon* are old men of Argos, too old to have accompanied Agamemnon on his expedition against Troy (72–82). They do not know that the watchman has seen the signal from the beacon.

Hail, beacon of the night that signals a light like day;
You will bring much dancing
To Argos in thanks for what has happened.

Look! Look! 25

This is my clear sign to Agamemnon's wife
To get out of bed and with all speed
Raise a cry of joyous welcome in the house for this fire-signal,
If the city of Ilium has been taken,
As the beacon clearly tells us. 30
I will make a start by dancing myself
From pleasure at my master's good fortune,
Since my beacon-watch has thrown me this triple six.
If only I may clasp in this hand
The kindly hand of the master of the house on his return. 35
As for the rest – I'll keep quiet. A great ox
Stands on my tongue, though the house itself, had it a voice,
Could speak most clearly. My words are meant for those
In the know. Those who are not will find me – forgetful.

(a) 40–103 *In veiled and metaphorical language the Chorus sing of the Greek expedition to punish Paris for abducting Helen and the Trojans for harbouring the couple. They speak of their own weakness and old age, then address Clytaemnestra, asking her why there are now sacrifices being made all over the city.*

Legal imagery

41 Priam's mighty prosecutors During the play the Trojan War is often spoken of as if it were a court case. The defendants are Paris, Priam and Troy; the prosecution Agamemnon and Menelaus, as agents of Zeus, god of hospitality (60–1, 348–9) and justice (356, 507). The charge is Paris' theft of Helen from his host Menelaus (see **Hospitality** page 8, lines 385–6), and Priam and Troy's subsequent harbouring of the couple; in addition, as king of Troy and head of the household (see **The house** page 2), Priam must answer for the actions of his son Paris. On the judge's bench are Zeus and Justice. The defendants are found guilty (515); the sentence is the destruction of Troy (516–17, 786–7), together with the deaths of Paris and Priam (802). Image becomes reality later in the *Oresteia* trilogy, which ends in a trial scene.

Zeus

44 Zeus A king's power traditionally derives from Zeus as king of the gods (*Iliad ii*, 100–8). In his omnipotence Zeus is ultimately responsible for ordering human affairs (1458–60): this belief is also expressed in the opening lines of the *Iliad*. Although his laws are unbending (1535–6), he is benign towards humankind (163–9), just (506–7) and protects the sacred laws (356–7).

Names for the Greeks

46 Argive At the time of the Trojan War, Argos is the largest territory in the Greek world and therefore the Greek force is often called 'Argive'. In the play the Greeks are variously called Argives, Danaans (63) and Achaeans (107) as they are in both the *Iliad* and the *Odyssey*. The use of these names adds epic resonance to the play.

48 a loud cry of War The text has 'Ares' not 'War': Ares is the god of war.

CHORUS   The tenth year this is   40
Since Priam's mighty prosecutors,
Kings Menelaus and Agamemnon, relentless pair of Atreidae,
Two thrones and two sceptres,
Honours from Zeus,
Sent from this land   45
The Argive fleet of a thousand ships,
A force to champion their cause,
Yelling a loud cry of War from the heart –

The Chorus, from the National Theatre production, London, 1981.

The language of the Chorus

49–54 Like vultures   The language and imagery that Aeschylus uses are often rich and complex, nowhere more so than in the choral odes (see **Legal imagery** page 6): images can work on several different levels (see notes on 404, 714 and 957; **An urgent warning** page 62), and at times the distinction between reality and image is blurred (421–7); there is also frequent use of metaphor, for example 'pulling at their winged oars' (52) for flying. Here the Chorus imagine that two vultures (the sons of Atreus) find that their young (Helen) have been stolen from their nest.

● What might this image for Helen suggest about the way a wife was viewed by the family into which she married? What other impressions does the image create?

55–6 high up some Apollo/Or Pan or Zeus   Apollo may be associated with birds in his role as god of prophecy, which often involves reading the flight of birds (see **Omens** page 14); Pan lives in wild countryside, including the mountains; Zeus lives on the heights of Mount Olympus and sees everything (see **Zeus** page 6).

The Furies

58 a Fury   The birds' cries cause one of the gods to send a Fury against the thief. The Furies (*Erinyes*) are goddesses of vengeance, most often for murder: they hound the victim's murderer and family until he is avenged. In the concluding play of this trilogy, the *Eumenides*, they form the Chorus. Here the Chorus see the Atreidae as avenging *Erinyes* sent by Zeus (60–2) to exact punishment from Paris for his abuse of hospitality (see below).

Hospitality

60 guardian of hospitality   The relationship between host and guest is accorded great importance in the Greek world and is sacred to Zeus (see **Zeus** page 6). A host is responsible for his guest; thus the guest owes a sacred obligation towards his host: together they are 'guest-friends'. This mutual obligation can be passed down the generations (in *Iliad vi*, 144–236 the Greek Diomedes encounters the Trojan Glaucus, but they do not fight as their fathers were guest-friends). Paris' breach of this relationship with Menelaus by his abduction of Helen ensures the righteousness of Agamemnon's cause (60) and helps justify eventual Trojan defeat (380–6).

62 much married   Helen marries Menelaus, then Paris; some legends also have her first marrying Theseus, and finally Paris' brother Deiphobus.

Like vultures high above their nests
Sorrowing for their young far from home, 50
Soaring, circling,
Pulling at their winged oars:
Their vigil over the nest,
Their exertion for their young – wasted.
But high up some Apollo 55
Or Pan or Zeus hearing the grief of his neighbours,
The shrill lament voiced by the birds,
Sends a Fury, to bring vengeance at last
Upon the transgressors.
So mighty Zeus, guardian of hospitality, 60
Sends the sons of Atreus after Paris
For the sake of a woman much married.

63 Danaans and Trojans alike   The Chorus stress the suffering endured by both the Danaans (see note on 46) and Trojans, a sentiment expressed often in the *Iliad* and in tragedy: there is no romantic notion that victory comes without suffering on both sides.

66 in the first engagements   That is, right from the start of the Trojan War. The Greek *proteleia* (first engagements) often refers to the rites preliminary to marriage, though Helen and Paris are already married (684–6) when the fighting starts.

69–70 Not with burnt offerings/Nor by pouring from unburnt libations   Offerings of food and drink are made to placate angry gods. The Chorus explain that in this case no offerings of any type will help avert the 'inexorable' anger of Zeus and the Furies (see **The Furies** page 8), who are angry at Paris' abuse of hospitality (60) in stealing Helen.

72 With no honour   The idea that war is where honour is won (106) is traditional: one of Homer's epithets for war is 'where men win glory'.

78 there is no fighting here   The text has 'nor is Ares at his post' (see note on 48).

80 on three feet   The Chorus mean their own two feet plus their staff. This image is found in the Sphinx's riddle solved by Oedipus: 'What has four feet in the morning, two at midday and three in the evening?' The answer is 'man': he crawls on all fours as a baby, walks on two feet in the prime of life and uses a stick as he grows old.

He inflicts the struggles on Danaans and Trojans alike,
Numerous and exhausting,
Knees strained in the dust, 65
Spear-shafts splintered in the first engagements.
Things are as they now are
And move towards fulfilment of their destiny.
Not with burnt offerings
Nor by pouring from unburnt libations 70
Will anyone charm away inexorable anger.

With no honour in our aged flesh,
Left behind at that time by the expedition,
We remain, propping our childlike strength
On our staffs. 75
The new marrow
Pushing up within our breasts
Is that of old men: there is no fighting here.
Extreme old age, its leaves already withering,
Makes its journey on three feet. 80
As unsteady as a child,
It drifts like a daydream.

A silent presence

83 But you, daughter of Tyndareus The Chorus address Clytaemnestra directly: this is the first reference to the possibility that she is on stage (see **Clytaemnestra's entrance** page 24). It is unusual for a character to enter unannounced (see **Character introduction** page 42, note on 1549) during a choral ode, but there are no absolute rules or conventions in the plays of fifth-century Athens. Clytaemnestra seems to be organising sacrifices (87, 91, 101) which are visible to them: she may therefore – possibly with attendants – be busy with rituals at altars on stage. The sacrifices are mentioned again (247, 575). Tyndareus is Clytaemnestra's father: her mother is Leda (see note on 887), who is also Helen's mother.

88 All the gods Various gods watch over the city: 'Those above' are those that live on Mount Olympus or elsewhere, 'those below' are the chthonic gods, those that live below in the Underworld.

90 the agora The market-place (*agora*) is the town centre where people shop, meet and pass the time. It is a public place and therefore its gods are contrasted with 'Those of the home'.

95 sacred oils Certain oils are valued for the soothing fragrance they give off when burnt, and are often used to accompany a sacrifice (see **Sacrifice** page 22), either to please the gods by their fragrance or to impress them that such a valuable substance is being burnt in their honour.

99–102 anxiety An atmosphere of anxiety already established by the watchman (1–9, 36–9) is now reinforced by the Chorus, even though they have explained that Zeus supports Agamemnon's case against Troy (60–1) and will ensure justice.

● Is it clear what the Chorus are anxious about?

But you, daughter of Tyndareus,
Queen Clytaemnestra,
What is it? What news? What have you heard? 85
What news do you trust that
You bid sacrifices be burned all around?
All the gods that watch over our city,
Those above, those below,
Those of the home, those of the agora – 90
All their altars burn with offerings.
In this direction and in that
Torch flames reach as high as the heavens,
Fed with the pure, soothing comfort
Of sacred oils 95
Mixed deep inside the palace.
Of these matters tell us
What you can and may,
And cure us of our anxiety,
Which at times rises malevolent; 100
But because of the sacrifices you now proclaim,
Hope is forcing back the insatiable worry
And the soul-destroying grief from my heart.

(b) 104–48 *The Chorus now sing of the Greek army as it sets out for Troy and the omen that occurs while it is assembled at the port of Aulis (see map, page x) waiting to board the ships: two eagles fly out and devour a pregnant hare. Calchas, the army prophet, interprets the omen and predicts that Artemis will demand a sacrifice in return for the dead hare.*

Metre

104–6 I have it in me … / … Persuasiveness/Breathes down on me
These words, like the invocations to the Muse at the opening of the *Iliad* and *Odyssey*, suggest poetic or prophetic inspiration, though the Chorus later imply that they themselves witnessed the events of which they speak (234). In the original Greek of lines 104–48 the Chorus use a *dactylic* metre similar to that of Homer, which gives their song epic resonance; lines 40–103 are *anapaests* – a sort of chanted, marching rhythm. The choral odes, however, are made up of a variety of metres, which are known collectively as *lyric*. The metre for ordinary dialogue in tragedy is *iambic*.

Omens

105 The fine omen Omens indicate the wishes of the gods: those skilled in reading them can discover the gods' will. Common omens are: the unusual behaviour of birds or animals; the sudden appearance of birds in the sky; thunder and lightning (especially in a clear sky). Many omens feature birds, perhaps because they live in the sky, just as the gods do. The eagle (111) is closely associated with Zeus because of its majesty (power, size and speed) and the fact that it is difficult to escape.

108 Hellas The Greek name for Greece as a whole, used from the seventh century BC to the present day.

109 Teucer was the first king of Troy.

113 on the right, the spear-side Birds flying on the right-hand side, the hand that holds the spear, constitute a favourable omen.

Optimism and pessimism

117 *Cry out, cry out in anguish, but may good prevail* The text has *ailinon*, a word uttered in lamentation: this refrain rounds off each of the three verses in this section of the *parodos* (117, 131, 148). The Chorus are often pessimistic (see note on 99–102; lines 439–56, 948–73), but make up for this with an overall optimism that Zeus (see **Zeus** page 6, lines 149–69, note on 164) and Justice (756) will ensure the proper outcome. Despite the overall positive nature of this omen, the choral refrain (117) expressing hope is also sensitive to the suffering anticipated in the violent destruction of the hare and her brood (see note on 121; lines 115, 122–30; **Optimism and pessimism** page 60).
● What are we to understand by 'good' (117, 131, 148)?

I have it in me to sing of a command over men in their prime and
    The fine omen on their journey, for still a divine Persuasiveness   105
Breathes down on me, though my old age leaves me fit for bravery
        Only in song. The twin-throned majesty of the Achaeans,
                Like-minded leaders of Hellas' youth,
Are sped on their way by a bird-omen against the land of Teucer,
                Hands of vengeance on their spears: 110
                A king of birds for each king of ships,
                    One dark, one white tailed.
        Appearing near the palace on the right, the spear-side,
                    They rest visible to all,
Feeding on a mother-hare, her swollen belly pregnant with young,   115
                    Cut short on her final dash.
        Cry out, cry out in anguish, but may good prevail.

Calchas

118 The army's noble seer   Calchas accompanies the army and interprets the gods' wishes. It is Calchas who explains at the start of the *Iliad* that Apollo is angry with the Achaeans: his explanation leads to the quarrel of Agamemnon and Achilles, which is the starting-point of events in that poem.

Meaning of the omen

121 In time this expedition   Calchas interprets the omen (121–4): the two eagles are the sons of Atreus (see note on 3) and they will feast on the hare (Troy) and its 'brood' (the Trojans). This suggests the terrible suffering of the Trojans, in particular the women and children within the city. The cruelty of this omen is like that in *Iliad ii*, 303–32, when a snake devours a sparrow and her young at the departure of the Greeks from Aulis for Troy.

125 may no divine malice   Calchas is worried that the gods may begrudge Greek success; thus at the outset of the expedition he has expressed his fears, fears that are echoed by the Chorus now during the *parodos* (see note on 99–102). The gods are thought to keep human success in check by causing the downfall of those who have too much of it (see **Resentment** page 40), just as the Greek army is now checking Troy for breaking the laws of man and god (see **Hospitality** page 8).

Artemis

127 holy Artemis   is daughter of Zeus and goddess of the hunt; despite this, she is also the protectress of animals (132–5). Like all the gods, she can try to oppose Zeus (128) or reach a compromise with him (136), but Zeus has ultimate power.

128 father's winged hunters   These are the eagles (111), called 'hunters' here because they hunt down the hare.

Apollo the Healer

138 I cry *i-ē* to Apollo the Healer!   Apollo is god of prophecy and healing. Perhaps the prophet Calchas addresses him as his patron or he may invoke Apollo in his capacity of 'Healer' because, as Artemis' brother, he may be able to assuage her anger. Apollo is frequently invoked by the cry 'i-ē'.

● Does Calchas imply that what happens is fixed or that Apollo can prevent it?

The army's noble seer watched them feasting on the hare
And took them for the two warlike Atreidae,
Twins in bravery, sovereign leaders, and he spoke 120
In prophecy thus: 'In time this expedition will take
The city of Priam and a violent doom
Will plunder the city's treasure,
All the heaped possessions in its towers.
But may no divine malice cast a shadow over 125
The great army forged to curb Troy;
For out of pity holy Artemis bears a grudge
Against her father's winged hunters
Which sacrifice the piteous hare and brood unborn;
She hates the eagles' feast.' 130
Cry out, cry out in anguish, but may good prevail.

'Such is the fair goddess' love
For the cubs of fierce lions, too dangerous to touch,
And such her delight too in the suckling young
Of all animals that roam the fields, 135
That she asks that these signs be fulfilled.
Favourable and yet flawed are the omens:
I cry *i-ē* to Apollo the Healer!

Sacrifice at Aulis
140 hold the ships back interminably   An omen at Aulis is
mentioned in the *Iliad* (see note on 121). The Chorus' version is
different, however: the fleet is delayed by adverse winds (see note on
173) and then Agamemnon's daughter Iphigeneia is sacrificed
(191–233).

A cycle of vengeance
141–4   Calchas speaks in grim terms of a 'second sacrifice' to come
(141); his prophecy is enigmatic, but he is referring to the sacrifice of
Iphigeneia; the first sacrifice was the dead hare (129) and now
Iphigeneia will be sacrificed as payment to Artemis for its death. This
second sacrifice becomes part of a cycle of vengeance and we hear in
cryptic terms of the 'discord' (142) it will cause and of a fearsome
individual back in the palace at Argos, the 'one/Who runs the house'
(142–3) who waits to take revenge for this sacrifice of a child (144).
Though this is the primary meaning, Iphigeneia is not the only child
whose death requires vengeance: it will later (1067–8) become
apparent that the children of Thyestes have yet to be avenged (see
Background to the story).

(c) **149–69**   *The Chorus break from events at Aulis to sing in praise of
Zeus and his willingness to help mankind reach understanding.*

Third generation of gods
156–60 Not even he   refers to Uranus and 'he who came next' to
Cronos. The first king of the gods, Uranus (*ouranos* means 'heavens')
is deposed by his son Cronos, who eats his own children to ensure
that he is not deposed in turn, but his youngest son Zeus is rescued
and grows up to overthrow his father. This story is told in the
Theogony by Hesiod, a contemporary of Homer, which describes a
powerful and just Zeus establishing order from primitive chaos.

160 Matched and thrown   The metaphor comes from a wrestling
match, in which one has to throw one's opponent three times to win.

Learning and suffering
164 his binding law   The Chorus are essentially optimistic (see
Optimism and pessimism page 14). They realise that men suffer for
their actions, but they believe that there is purpose in this suffering:
men will learn from it. Out of this learning process come
understanding (162–3) and knowledge.

169 bench   The image is of the helmsman guiding the ship as he sits
on his bench; in the same way the gods guide mankind to
understanding.

Let her not cause the winds to blow against the Danaans,
    To hold the ships back interminably without sailing,   140
Nor hasten a second sacrifice, without feasting, without music,
    Born to create discord, afraid of no man. For the one
Who runs the house, formidable and deceitful, is waiting
To rise up again: child-avenging Anger that will not forget.'
Such fateful events did Calchas cry out to the royal house   145
    Together with great blessings as he read the birds
      Along the journey; in accord with this
    Cry out, cry out in anguish, but may good prevail.

    Zeus, whosoever he may be, if by this name
      He is pleased to be invoked,   150
      By this I address him:
    I cannot – as I weigh in the balance all things –
      Compare anything with Zeus,
      When there is true need
    To throw off the vain burden of anxiety;   155

    Not even he who was great in times past,
      Bursting with belligerent audacity,
    He shall not be spoken of: he is no more;
      And he who came next is gone,
      Matched and thrown three times.   160
But Zeus – whoever cries out a loyal victory-song to him
    Shall reach complete understanding.

He set mortals on the road to understanding,
He made 'Learning comes through suffering' his binding law.
      Pain that recalls past woes   165
    Drips into our hearts while we sleep;
Even the unwilling come to understand this.
    The gods force this kindness on us
    As they sit at their august bench.

(d) 170–243 *The Chorus return to events at Aulis: Agamemnon's response to Calchas' interpretation of the omen, his dilemma and his eventual decision. However, they stop short of describing events to their conclusion. The* parodos *proper ends with expressions of fear: the Chorus know that the bulk of Calchas' prophecy has come true (139–42), but are reluctant to think about the final part (142–4) of it.*

173 Added his breath to this adverse wind Agamemnon takes no action to help the fleet, in effect assisting the adverse winds to keep the ships penned at Aulis.

176–8 Chalcis … Aulis … Strymon See map on page x.

185 A remedy yet more grim The Chorus do not explain the remedy themselves.

● Why do the Chorus choose to explain Calchas' remedy through Agamemnon's words (192–203) rather than their own?

188–9 beating/The ground This gesture of discontent is also found in *Odyssey ii.*

196 a daughter's Iphigeneia, who was at home at Argos, had to be summoned to Aulis. In one version of the story (Euripides' play *Iphigeneia at Aulis*), Agamemnon summons her on the pretext that she is to be married to Achilles, the greatest of the Greek warriors who went to Troy.

200 It is right for you to insist It would be right and proper for the chiefs to be angry if Agamemnon refuses to sacrifice Iphigeneia and instead betrays the fleet (198–9) by cancelling the expedition against Troy.

And then the elder commander   170
Of the Achaean ships,
Blaming no prophet,
Added his breath to this adverse wind,
While the Achaean army
Laboured: no sailing, supplies diminishing,   175
Stuck opposite Chalcis
On the beaches of Aulis which echo to the roar.

There blew in from Strymon winds of
Hunger, ill-mooring, foul idleness
Causing the men to stray,   180
Merciless to cables and ships:
They made time twice as long,
Wearing down, tearing at the flower of the Argives.
But then the seer cried out to the leaders
A remedy yet more grim   185
Than the bitter weather,
Citing Artemis.
The Atreidae, beating
The ground with their staffs, did not
Hold back their tears.   190

And then the sovereign king replied:
'Heavy is my heart if I do not obey,
Heavy too, if
I butcher my child, pride of my house,
Smearing a father's hands   195
In a daughter's blood-bath at the altar.

Is either course without evil?
How can I become traitor to the fleet,
Fail the alliance?
It is right for you to insist   200
In angry frustration
On a sacrifice of virgin blood to calm the winds.
May good come of it.'

Agamemnon's dilemma

204 he buckled on the harness of necessity Agamemnon faces a tragic dilemma, for he cannot fulfil both his public duty as a commander and private duty as a father: whatever action he takes, he will do wrong. The Chorus use an image of an ox attached to a yoke by means of a harness, to illustrate how Agamemnon (the ox) is tied to necessity (the yoke) by means of his actions (the harness).

- What factors must Agamemnon take into account when deciding whether to sacrifice Iphigeneia?
- Does it seem that Agamemnon truly has a choice?

Sacrifice

210 to be the one to sacrifice Sacrifice is a common ritual of Greek community life and has two main purposes: to thank the gods for their help or to ask them for it. Sacrifices follow a routine: an animal (usually domesticated) is sprinkled with corn and wine, and led to be sacrificed (it must appear to go willingly), perhaps by a priest on the altar in front of a temple or the head of the household (see **The house** page 2) at the altar in the home. The animal is then killed, its blood is collected and poured onto the ground; the edible meat is cooked and shared out, the inedible parts (mainly the bones and the fat) are burnt for the gods to enjoy the savour of the roasting, which might be enhanced by aromatic oils (see note on 95). For Agamemnon to treat his own daughter like a sacrificial animal is 'evil', 'unholy' and sacrilegious (205–9). He ignores her prayers (214), muzzles her (221) and stifles her cries: all of this would mark him out for inevitable justice (236).

212 a woman Helen.

228 Like the subject of a painting The Chorus imagine that while looking at a painting, their eyes are automatically drawn to the character at its centre, who seems on the verge of speaking. In the same way the eyes of those present at the sacrifice are drawn to Iphigeneia as she tries to speak.

- Does the vividness of the language suggest the Chorus were present at the sacrifice (234)?

230–1 at her father's house/In the men's lavish quarters A reference to a royal girl in the men's quarters of the palace is surprising. Respectable women or girls would not appear there, whether to sing the traditional hymn to Apollo at the end of the meal or for any other reason.

- What is the effect of this detail in the narrative?

232 libation A libation is an offering of liquid to the gods. All or part of the liquid (wine, milk, olive oil or honey) is poured onto the ground or an altar. The third libation (see **A thank-offering to Zeus** page 102) is reserved for Zeus.

But when he buckled on the harness of necessity,
And blew his thoughts down an evil course,   205
Unholy, unsacred – from that moment
He set his mind on boundless audacity.
For such derangement emboldens men –
Wretched, evil thinking, seed of sorrow;
And so he brought himself to be the one to sacrifice   210
His daughter, to safeguard
A war of vengeance over a woman,
A first sacrifice for the fleet.

Her prayers, her cries of 'father',
Her innocent youth, the leaders,   215
Intent on war, valued at nothing;
After a prayer her father told his attendants
To lift her like a goat
Face downwards over the altar
– As she fell about his robes in desperation –   220
And with a muzzle over the soft curve
Of her mouth to prevent
Any utterance, any curse on the house.

She waits voiceless under constraint of the gag;
As her saffron-dyed robe trailed down,   225
She hit each of the sacrificers
With a pitiable shot from her eye,
Like the subject of a painting
Ever wishing to speak,
For she had often sung to them at her father's house   230
In the men's lavish quarters, still unviolated and with pure voice;
As her beloved father poured the third libation, she would lovingly
Sing Apollo's joyous hymn.

The future

234–40 The Chorus will not sing about the sacrifice itself or any of the events of the Trojan War. They accept that the future is predetermined, that Calchas is able to read it and that there is yet suffering to come, as Calchas had predicted (144). However, they feel that to harbour gloomy thoughts is unnecessary – what will come, will come (238).

The scales of Justice

236 Justice tilts The image is of a pair of pan scales, held by Justice (here personified, see **Impersonal forces** page 34). The pan with the heavier weight drops – this signifies suffering and learning, though the Chorus do not specify for whom. It was Zeus who introduced the principle that mortals learn by suffering (164), so in saying that Justice enforces this law, the Chorus associate Zeus with Justice (see **Zeus and Justice** page 32).

Clytaemnestra's entrance

242 the sole guardian The Chorus may wish this to serve as a complimentary greeting, for it is not clear when Clytaemnestra enters (see **A silent presence** page 12). It is possible that she may have left the stage and re-enters now.

○ Consider the dramatic effect of Clytaemnestra's presence onstage during the *parodos*, especially if she is lighting the fires of sacrifice (see **A silent presence** page 12).

○ Is there anything in the *parodos* which it could be important for her to hear?

243 Argos The text has *Apia*, an alternative name for Argos. Apis was a mythical king of Argos.

Further points to consider about the *parodos* (40–243)

● The Chorus sing of events that happened at Aulis ten years previously. What might be their significance now?

● What attitude do they display towards those events: do they pass any judgement on Artemis' actions or on Agamemnon's?

Staging the *parodos*

○ How might such a long choral ode be staged? Would you have some lines sung in unison and some individually? Which parts would be more suited to musical accompaniment? Do some sections require special emphasis? Which parts could be made clearer with actions?

I neither saw nor speak of events after that;
The arts of Calchas are not without fulfilment,   235
Justice tilts against those who are to learn
By suffering. As for the future,
You will hear it as it happens. Before then, leave well alone;
To do otherwise is to grieve too soon:
Conspicuous in the early morning light the future will arrive.   240
May what follows from here turn out well,
In line with the wishes of the sole guardian
Of the land of Argos, her champion closest to hand.

*In a sacrifice similar to that of Iphigeneia, the Trojan
princess Polyxena is sacrificed to honour the dead
Achilles. Black-figure Tyrrhenian amphora (c. 570 BC).*

FIRST EPISODE (244–340)

Clytaemnestra tells the Chorus that Troy has been captured. She explains how she comes to know this so quickly, then she describes the scene at the fallen city as she imagines it.

Authority

244 respect for your authority In ancient Greece it would have been most unusual for a woman to be given any authority (*kratos*) outside the home (see **Male and female** page 2); in the absence of the head of the household (see **The house** page 2), authority would pass to a male relative; in the absence of the king, authority would pass to a suitable man or council of men. The Chorus tell Clytaemnestra outright that they only give her obeisance because Agamemnon is away.

○ Consider the appearance of Clytaemnestra. Might she be wearing trappings associated with authority or sacrifice (see **A silent presence** page 12)?

247 you are busy with sacrifices See **A silent presence** page 12, **Clytaemnestra's entrance** page 24.

Stichomythia (254–66)

A passage where the characters speak alternate lines in a quick-fire exchange is called *stichomythia*. It is often found when one character needs to obtain information from another or when two characters argue.

● How does *stichomythia* help to establish the character of Clytaemnestra and the Chorus' attitude towards her?

● Why does Aeschylus use *stichomythia* at this point?

The beacon speech

267–302 *Clytaemnestra has stationed watchmen in a chain from Troy across to Argos. When Troy falls, the watchman on Lemnos sees the flames and lights the fire of his beacon, which is in turn seen by the watchman on Mount Athos, who in turn lights his fire and so on, until the flame arrives in Argos. Clytaemnestra mentions several places now unknown: those whose location is known are marked on the map, page x.*

267 Hephaestus is the god of fire and metalwork, in the *Iliad* lame, but a quick metaphorical messenger here. **Ida** is a mountain near Troy: in the *Iliad* the gods sit on it to watch the Trojan War.

270 Mount Athos is one of the largest mountains in Greece and therefore fit for the king of the gods.

I am here out of respect for your authority, Clytaemnestra:
It is right to defer to a ruler's wife, when the throne 245
Is bereft of its male occupant. In all goodwill I would like to hear
Whether you are busy with sacrifices because you have heard
Reliable news, or in the hope of something good;
Though if you are silent, there will be no offence.

CLYTAEMNESTRA May dawn, as the proverb goes, 250
Bring good news from her kindly mother night.
You are about to learn of joy beyond hope:
The Argives have taken Priam's city.

CHORUS What's that you say? In disbelief your words escaped me.
CLYTAEMNESTRA Troy is in Greek hands; do I make myself clear? 255
CHORUS Joy steals up on me, calling forth tears.
CLYTAEMNESTRA Yes, your eyes prove your loyal thoughts.
CHORUS What makes you so sure? Have you proof of this?
CLYTAEMNESTRA I have: of course. Unless the god plays tricks.
CHORUS Are you relying on something you saw in a dream? 260
CLYTAEMNESTRA I would not clutch at something I saw in my sleep.
CHORUS Then has some unfledged rumour fed your hopes?
CLYTAEMNESTRA You take me for a child and insult my intelligence.
CHORUS So how long is it since the city was sacked?
CLYTAEMNESTRA Last night, I say, parent to this very day. 265
CHORUS And who could reach us with this news so fast?
CLYTAEMNESTRA Hephaestus, sending a blazing light from Ida:
From that first courier-fire, beacon sent beacon all the way here.
From Ida to the rock of Hermes on Lemnos,
From that island Zeus' Mount Athos 270
Received the mighty torch third.
It rises high as if riding the waves,
The power of fire on its journey of joy.
The pine, burning gold like the sun,
Announced its flame to the look-outs at Makistos. 275
No hesitation then, no inadvertent succumbing
To sleep or neglect of its share of the messenger's work;
From far off the light of the beacon signals its approach
Over the streams of Euripus to the watchmen of Messapion.

300 The first runner gains the victory, as does the last   The first beacon and the last beacon play an equal part in the success or 'victory' of the message reaching Clytaemnestra as planned. The original Athenian audience would have witnessed an actual torch relay race, for there was one in the *Panathenaia* festival held at Athens each year.

A powerful speech
301 Such a signal is proof
- What effect might Clytaemnestra intend her speech (267–302) to have on the Chorus? Does it answer their doubts and criticisms (254–66)?
- What does the speech reveal about Clytaemnestra's character?
- What might the Chorus find marvellous (304) about the speech?
- Why might it be so important for Clytaemnestra to arrange such quick news of Troy's fall?

The scene at Troy
306–23   Given that she is unlikely to have first-hand experience of such a scene, Clytaemnestra contrasts the fortunes of the defeated Trojans (312–15) with those of the Achaean victors (316–23) in powerful language and with impressive insight.

They shone back in answer and passed the message on further, 280
Setting alight the heap of grey bracken.
That mighty flame, as yet undimmed,
Leaping across the plain of Asopus
Towards the crag of Cithaeron, glowing like the moon,
Sparked another relay of messenger-fire. 285
Nor did the look-out ignore that light sent from afar,
Burning still brighter than those before;
His light darted across lake Gorgopis,
And, reaching the mountain where the goats roam,
Urged the mandate of fire not to fail. 290
They kindle and send out a great beard of flame:
In its unstinting might it passes the conspicuous headland
Of the Saronic Gulf and flames onwards.
Then it swooped down to arrive at
The crag of Arachnaeon, the watch-tower near the city; 295
And then it leaps to this, the roof of the Atreidae,
This flame, direct descendant from the fire of Ida.
This then was my system for relaying the torches,
One after another, discharged in sequence;
The first runner gains the victory, as does the last. 300
Such a signal is proof, I tell you,
Of my husband sending news from Troy to me.
CHORUS I will offer prayers to the gods once more, my lady;
But I would like to hear your tale and marvel at it,
From start to finish – if you would tell it again. 305
CLYTAEMNESTRA The Achaeans hold Troy on this very day:
I can imagine the conflicting cries that sound within the city.
When you pour oil and vinegar in the same vessel,
You would not call them friends – they go their separate ways.
So too one can hear the voices of conquered 310
And conqueror, quite separate in their dual fortune:
The conquered collapse around the bodies
Of husbands and brothers, and children fall
Around their old fathers: necks now in thrall,
They lament the death of those dearest to them. 315

Potential dangers

324–33 if they respect Clytaemnestra now expresses her awareness that even though Troy has been conquered, there are still several pitfalls awaiting the victorious Achaeans before they are safely home. They must not harm the sacred buildings in Troy (325); they must not take inappropriate plunder (328). She believes that spirits of the dead (332) have the power to cause harm: the Trojan dead, the Greek dead and even the dead Iphigeneia may all have a grievance against Agamemnon and the army. Finally, there is always the chance that some unforeseen disaster may occur (333).

Male and female

334 from me, a woman The Chorus have stated that they only give Clytaemnestra respect because she is the king's wife (245–6), and even then their respect has not been absolute, since at first they are reluctant to believe her news and have questioned her credibility (254–66). Clytaemnestra may mean this remark to be a pointed reply to their doubting her because she is a woman. The Chorus reply that skill in speaking is a male attribute (337).

335 May good prevail Clytaemnestra uses the same phrasing as the Chorus (see **Optimism and pessimism** page 14).

● Do you think her view of 'good' is the same as that of the Chorus?

336 For I have chosen Clytaemnestra's final remark is obscure.

● Why might Clytaemnestra wish to end on such a cryptic note?

340 the reward is the plundering of the city; **that hard toil** is the fighting at Troy.

Clytaemnestra's first scene (244–340)

● What attitude do the Chorus adopt in Clytaemnestra's presence?
● What impression does she generate by her two powerful speeches? How does she convince the Chorus that she should be believed after they have doubted her (254–66)?
● What is the overall tone of her second speech? Does she celebrate the victory at Troy?
● Clytaemnestra claims she speaks as a woman (334). Does she say anything that might stem from a woman's viewpoint?

Clytaemnestra's exit

It is not clear whether Clytaemnestra goes inside the palace at line 340 (see **A silent presence** page 12). If she does, she has to return near the end of the First *Stasimon*, for she speaks as soon as the Chorus have finished singing (470), and is very quick to see a herald approaching (474).

And the conquerors – after the battle
The exertion of night prowling sets them hungry to what breakfast
The city can muster, according to no mark of rank,
But as each drew his fortune's lot.
Released from the frozen dew under the open sky   320
Now they occupy their Trojan prisoners' homes,
And like men at ease they sleep
The whole night through without a guard.
Now, if they respect the gods of the captive land
Who protect the city and the temples of those gods,   325
Then the conquerors may not in their turn be caught.
So may no desire assail the army first
To plunder what they should not, overcome by their loot.
They must make the return journey home in safety,
Wheeling back round on the return leg of the course.   330
Even if the army travels without offence to the gods,
The grief of the dead may be awakened
Or some sudden misfortune take place.
You hear all this from me, a woman.
May good prevail, unmistakable for all to see: 335
For I have chosen to gain from these many blessings.
CHORUS My lady, you speak thoughtfully and like a man of sense.
Now I have heard your compelling proofs,
I am readying myself to call upon the gods,
As the reward gained for that hard toil is no mean one.   340

FIRST CHORAL ODE (1ST *STASIMON*) (341–469)

A stasimon *is a choral ode and comes at the end of an episode. In the course of this ode the Chorus tell the story of Paris' abduction of Helen to Troy, but they reflect upon these events in generalising moral terms. In the first part of the ode (341–86) the Chorus react to the news that Troy has been sacked and consider the part played by Paris; in the second part (387–438) they recall the effect that Helen's abduction had on Menelaus and the consequences of the war for the people of Greece; they conclude that it is better not to be spoken of too highly (450–1), for then one is not resented for one's success. What begins as a triumphal hymn ends in apprehension typical of the Chorus (see note on 99–102, **Optimism and pessimism** page 14).*

341 kindly Night   Night is described as 'kindly' because it has brought many blessings, both the sack of Troy itself and the Chorus' learning of it; the 'great finery' (342) may be a general reference to the array of stars each night or refer specifically to the Trojan possessions won during the previous night.

The net

344 A covering net   The image is from hunting: once enmeshed in the net, the quarry cannot escape. Zeus tracks Paris down and aims his bow at him (350–1). The notion that it is impossible to escape from out of the net will reappear later in the play (1086, 1346, 1353).

Zeus and Justice

356 The gods do not deign to care   The Chorus attribute the destruction of Troy to Zeus (349), god of hospitality (348), as a punishment for Paris' crime (350). Others may question whether the gods are interested in human affairs, but the Chorus see that Zeus will punish the transgressor (355–61), whether immediately, in the near future or even after the transgressor's death: if a wrongdoer escapes punishment at the time, it follows that his descendants will have to pay for his crime (359, **The cause of wickedness** page 58). Those who violate the altar of Justice (369) are bound to suffer (see note on 164, lines 236–7, **The scales of Justice** page 24).

367 Excess   See **Impersonal forces** page 34, **Resentment** page 40.

Zeus, king, and kindly Night,
Possessor of great finery,
You have thrown over the towers of Troy
A covering net, so neither the mighty
Nor even the young might get clear of   345
That great mesh of slavery
And all-catching destruction.
I revere Zeus, great god of hospitality:
He it was accomplished this,
He stretched his bow against Paris long since,   350
So the arrow would not fly in vain,
Neither short of the mark nor beyond the stars.

They can speak of a blow from Zeus
And follow the trail this far, to see that
He achieved what he ordained. Some man said   355
The gods do not deign to care about mortals
Who trample on the beauty of holy things:
But he was no pious man.
Revealed to that man's descendants
Is the price for recklessness   360
And for adopting greater airs than is right:
Extravagance fills his halls,
Beyond what is best. My prayer is for
A life free from harm, such as would satisfy
A man of good sense.   365
Wealth is no safeguard
Against Excess
For the man who kicks the great
Altar of Justice into oblivion.

Impersonal forces

370 Tireless Persuasion The Chorus have declared their belief in the traditional Olympian gods: Zeus, Apollo, Ares, Artemis (and others later in the play). However, they also acknowledge an array of other dark and powerful forces – personified, though not anthropomorphic, concepts such as Persuasion (*Peithō* 370), Destruction or Ruin (*Atē* 347, 371, 712, 746), Justice (*Dikē* 236, 369), Excess (*Koros* 367), Wrath (*Mēnis* 678) and a dark spirit known as a *daimōn* (see **Daimōn** page 58), as well as the Furies (*Erinyes*, see **The Furies** page 8, 445, 725) and later in the play Strife (*Eris* 677, 1434). Often these forces are agents of Zeus, but they do not always work explicitly under his direction.

Paris' responsibility

371 child of Destruction Destruction (*Atē*) personified (see above) plans the destruction of a man, then her daughter Persuasion (*Peithō*) makes their victim commit a crime: whether he perceives it or not, the victim has no choice (372), yet he must still take responsibility for his actions (377, 380–2). In the *parodos* a similar notion pertained to Agamemnon (see note on 204); in this passage (374–86) it becomes clear that this applies specifically to Paris (he is not named in the Greek), who was beguiled into abducting Helen.

374 base bronze The true composition of a bronze object is soon exposed after a few knocks and scrapes: if the bronze is not pure, the black of its impurity shows through. In the same way, when Paris is put to the test and judged, his evil nature is uncovered (376).

379 chasing after a flying bird To try to catch a flying bird is to attempt the impossible. Paris has put a blight on Troy by shaming the table of hospitality (385); it will be impossible for him to escape justice, despite his attempts.

384 home of the Atreidae This phrase, used before of Agamemnon's palace at Argos (3), here denotes Menelaus' palace at Sparta.

● What is the effect of linking the two brothers so closely?

Tireless Persuasion is compelling –   370
She is the inexorable child of Destruction who schemes ahead.
All remedy is vain; their mischief is not hidden
But plain, a dread-blazing light.
As when base bronze
Is rubbed and knocked,   375
Through such trial an ingrained blackness
Is revealed. Paris placed
On his city an impossible burden,
Like a boy chasing after a flying bird.
None of the gods hears his entreaty,   380
Instead they destroy the unjust man
Who has turned to such ways.
Even such was Paris: entering
The home of the Atreidae,
He shamed the table of hospitality   385
By his theft of its mistress.

The cost of war (387–456)

*The Chorus now sing of Helen's abduction ten years before, which brings grief first to Menelaus (394–410), then to the people of Greece (413–38) and Troy (390). The womenfolk send their men out from their homes alive and well, but are given back cremated ashes (413–27); the resentment of the people begins to stir against Agamemnon and Menelaus, that so many have died for the sake of one woman (428–38, note on 431). The sons of Atreus may have won a triumphant victory but only at the cost of their popularity: the Chorus would rather live the ordinary life (450–6) that causes no resentment (see **Resentment** page 40).*

393 spokesmen   Menelaus sits in silence and alone in his palace at Sparta (397) – the Chorus use direct speech to convey grief and despair, just as they did for Agamemnon's reaction to Calchas' remedy for the adverse winds at Aulis (see note on 185).

- What is the effect of Menelaus' silence?
- What is the effect of a third party (the 'spokesmen') reporting Menelaus' emotions as they observe them?

399 a ghost

- Why do you think the spokesmen describe Menelaus in this way?

402 emptiness of their eyes   For all that the palace statues of Helen or others are beautiful, when Menelaus looks into their lifeless eyes, he feels his loss all the more. This emptiness forms a poignant contrast with the eloquence of Iphigeneia's glance before she is sacrificed (227).

403 Aphrodite   The goddess of love; here she perhaps represents Menelaus' happiness because of his love for Helen, rather than love or desire itself.

Grief

404 Grief-stricken images   Menelaus' images of Helen are tinged with his own grief at her absence; he may also be dreaming that Helen herself is stricken with grief over her actions, which in turn brought grief to Menelaus, Sparta (387) and the womenfolk of Greece as a whole (see above).

- Does Menelaus' grief seem less important when compared to that of Sparta and the womenfolk of Greece (416–31)?

She left behind for her townspeople a throng
Of shield-bearers, the forming of squadrons
And the arming of sailors,
And took to Ilium destruction as her dowry,   390
As she stepped lightly through the gate,
Daring what she should not; and much they grieved,
The spokesmen of her house, as they said:
'Alas, alas for the house, for the house and its masters,
Alas for the marriage-bed and the haunts of a loving wife;   395
Here now is silence, dishonoured, unprotesting,
Incredulous, sitting apart for all to see;
In longing for her overseas
It will seem that a ghost rules the halls;
The beauty of graceful statues   400
Gives no joy to her husband:
In the emptiness of their eyes
All Aphrodite drains away.

Grief-stricken images
Appear in his dreams but afford   405
Vain satisfaction.
For in vain does a man glimpse what seems lovely:
Slipping away through his hands
The vision is gone; with no pause
It follows on its wings down the paths of sleep.'   410
Such are the sorrows at the hearth in her house,
Such they are and more beyond these.
Everywhere in every home of those who went with him
From the land of Hellas, there is plain to see
A sorrowing woman with steadfast heart.   415
Ah – it cuts to the quick.
For she knows the man
She sent out; but back to each man's home
Instead of men
Come urns and ash.   420

421 Ares, gold-broker in bodies Ares, god of war, exchanges men for ashes as a gold-changer exchanges valuables for gold-dust; both use scales to weigh out the appropriate amount. Ares' gold may also be the plunder that war can bring.

- What is the effect of this image from the world of trade?

431 For the sake of another man's wife Similar observations are made several times in the play (62, 212, 798, 1426).

- Do you think it is implied that it was not worth fighting such a costly war over a woman?

434 The Atreidae as they pursue their case The sons of Atreus prosecute their case for Helen's return (see **Legal imagery** page 6).

435 there around the wall The Greek dead lie in the ground they won near the walls of Troy, but hate the earth that, now dead, they are forced to embrace.

The Chorus' concerns

439–56 The Chorus express several concerns. First, the people of Greece (413–14) curse the sons of Atreus and their curses require fulfilment; the strength of the citizens' anger will ensure that they are indeed fulfilled (440) – that the debt incurred by them is paid. Secondly, the Chorus know that the gods may punish Agamemnon, because he is responsible for a great number of deaths, even though in war this is an inevitable consequence of being a commander; Agamemnon had no choice, but still must accept responsibility (see **Paris' responsibility** page 34). Thirdly, they now seem worried (perhaps with Iphigeneia's sacrifice in mind) that Agamemnon may have prospered unjustly (446) and have doubts about the means (her sacrifice) to the end (the sack of Troy). This leads them to their final concern, that his success at Troy may incur the resentment (see **Resentment** page 40) of the gods.

- Do the Chorus seem to include themselves among those who lost relatives in the Trojan War and who resent the Atreidae for it?

449 unseen is the literal meaning of 'Hades' (the Underworld) and here refers to the inhabitants of Hades – the dead.

Ares, gold-broker in bodies,
Who holds the scales in the spear-fight,
From the pyres at Ilium
Sends back to their loved ones
A measure of dust and tears,   425
Cramming the urns with ash – a man once,
Now easy to pack in.
They grieve while they praise,
How this man was skilled in battle,
How that one fell honourably in the carnage –   430
For the sake of another man's wife.
Someone growls such things in secret
And bitter resentment creeps after
The Atreidae as they pursue their case.
But there around the wall   435
Others in their prime occupy
Tombs of Ilian earth; the land they hate
Shrouds its conquerors.

Anger in citizens' talk is dangerous:
It settles the debt of the curses the people have uttered.   440
I wait with misgiving to hear
What is hidden in darkness.
For the gods do not overlook
Mass-killers;
In time, the dark Furies erase the life of a man   445
Who has prospered unjustly,
Reversing his fortune,
Placing him in obscurity;
He has no defence as he goes down amongst the unseen.

Resentment

453 I choose unresented happiness The Chorus prefer to avoid success and the attention it brings from the gods, who resent it. The Chorus believe that the best course for humans is the ordinary life (454–6). To go beyond the ordinary is dangerous: the man who goes too far is guilty of arrogance (*hubris*) or excess (*koros*) and will incur the resentment (*phthonos*) of the gods and his fellow men. The gods will punish such a man with ruin or death, either themselves or by sending a Fury (445) or another of the impersonal powers (see **Impersonal forces** page 34) – usually Destruction (*Atē*). Often in tragedy the ordinary characters declare their desire for a life of moderation, usually in response to the ruin visited upon their superiors.

Doubts resurface (457–69)

The Chorus offer three points of view. The first is that there has not yet been satisfactory confirmation of the rumour sweeping Argos that Troy has been sacked (460); the second is that only a fool would be convinced by a beacon-signal and then be disappointed when it is found to be false (461–4); the third is that the news is unreliable because it has come from a woman (465–9).

Glory

469 Glory proclaimed by a woman A man's glory (*kleos*, a word found often in Homer) is what he has done that is great and worthy of fame: here Agamemnon's sack of Troy. The Chorus continue to cast aspersions on the credibility of women (see **Male and female** page 30).

- If Clytaemnestra now enters (see **Clytaemnestra's exit** page 30), does it matter whether she hears this remark (see **Male and female** page 48)?

First *Stasimon* (341–469)

The *stasimon* starts with the celebration of the punishment of Paris, but culminates in the Chorus' melancholy thoughts on divine retribution; it finishes with doubts about Clytaemnestra's news.

- Trace the subject-matter through the *stasimon*. Is it possible to find some logical progression in the Chorus' thoughts and thus understand how their initial joy turns to fear and doubt? What in fact do the Chorus fear?
- Why do the Chorus continue to sing of events ten years ago? Does the *stasimon* advance our understanding of the background to the Trojan War? Are any parts of it relevant to the previous scene?
- Consider how the *stasimon* might be staged for a modern audience, unfamiliar with the story and unused to such complex expression, through each part in turn.

To be spoken of too highly   450
Is dangerous: the thunderbolt of Zeus
Is thrown at such a man's house.
I choose unresented happiness:
May I never be a sacker of cities
            Nor myself know life   455
As a captive in the power of another.

        – The fire and its good news
            Send a swift rumour
Through the city: whether it is true,
Who knows? Does it come from the gods or is it a lie?   460
    – Who is so naïve or whose wits so deranged,
That he lets his heart be inflamed by news
            From signals of fire, but is then
Disappointed if their meaning turns out differently?
        – It is typical of a woman's impulse   465
To approve a thanksgiving before all is revealed.
            Female convictions are fickle,
            Apt to shift and change quickly;
Glory proclaimed by a woman fades and dies quickly.

SECOND EPISODE (470–661)

A herald arrives from Troy with details of the city's capture. He admits he is relieved to be back alive and stresses the justice of the Greek cause (484–518); he then tells of the struggle at Troy (532–63). After Clytaemnestra gives her reaction to his report and in response to the Chorus' enquiry, the herald recounts the storm on the journey home that separated Menelaus from Agamemnon and the rest of the fleet (617–61).

470 Soon we shall know For over two hundred lines (336–567), Clytaemnestra gives this speech only: some editors therefore assign the speech to the Chorus. If she is present (see **Clytaemnestra's exit** page 30), the herald certainly does not acknowledge her.

● Do you think these words are better suited to Clytaemnestra or to the Chorus?

Character introduction
474 I see a herald A character in tragedy is usually introduced before his or her arrival, to help the audience. The wearing of an olive-wreath (475) indicates good news.

Passing of time
484 Hail, ancestral earth It is a convention of tragedy that 'real time' is suspended during a play, and time may pass more quickly (particularly during a choral ode) than would actually be possible; the action of most tragedies takes place over a single day. Thus it is that over the space of a *stasimon* a herald, and later Agamemnon himself, can travel from Troy to Argos.

Homecoming
485 I have returned The homecoming (*nostos*) of a hero is an important theme in epic poetry and can be what makes the sufferings of war and travel worthwhile. Stories of the homecoming of the heroes from Troy, like the delayed return of Menelaus (see note on 599), were well known, the most famous being the story of Odysseus' *nostos* told in the *Odyssey*. The homecoming of the hero also brings relief to those who may have suffered during his absence (503–4, 582–5). Though the herald does not have heroic status, his words and sentiments embody these ideas.

Pythian Apollo
490–1 Pythian lord!/Shoot arrows at us The Pythian lord is Apollo, so-called because he slew an enormous python at Delphi, which then became the shrine of his oracle; the priestess there is known as the *Pythia.* The herald may be alluding to the episode at the start of the *Iliad* in which Apollo shoots plague-arrows at the Achaean army because Agamemnon has dishonoured his priest. He is invoked as 'healer' (see **Apollo the Healer**, page 16); perhaps the herald hopes he will heal the wounds caused by the Trojan War.

CLYTAEMNESTRA Soon we shall know about the light-bearing   470
  Torches and exchanges of beacon-signal and fire.
  Whether they are true, or like a dream,
  Their welcome light came to trick our senses.
  I see a herald here from the coast, his brow shaded
  By an olive-wreath: that parched dust and mud   475
  Side by side like sisters are my evidence.
  He is not mute, he will not light you a fire
  Of mountain wood and signal his message by fiery smoke.
  No, either his words will proclaim the celebrations more clearly,
  Or... But I have no desire for the opposite news –   480
  May his prove a welcome addition to what already bodes well.
CHORUS May whoever prays that things be otherwise for this city
  Reap the fruits of his wayward thinking.
HERALD Hail, ancestral earth of the land of Argos,
  On this day in the tenth year I have returned,   485
  Fulfilling at least one of many hopes that were broken;
  For I was never confident that I would die here
  And receive my due, the burial in Argive soil I so longed for.
  Now hail, my land, hail, light of the sun,
  Hail, Zeus supreme over the land and hail, Pythian lord!   490
  Shoot arrows at us from your bow no more:

492 Scamander's banks The Scamander is a river near Troy.

494–5 the gods/Of the assembly The assembly (see note on 819) is where matters of state are discussed.

496 Hermes is the patron of heralds because he is the messenger god.

497 the heroes who sent us out These are the ghosts of Argive heroes from the past, who are thought to watch over the army as it leaves Argos and then protect it on the journey.

500 Holy seats and gods who face the sun Outside the palace are special seats where royalty sit when conducting affairs of state outdoors. The 'gods who face the sun' refers to the gods' statues situated outside the palace: in the light of the sun their eyes appear to shine (502).

506–7 the mattock/Of Zeus that brings justice Agamemnon is said to demolish Troy with Zeus' mattock, because Zeus oversees the city's destruction to ensure justice for the theft of Helen (see **Zeus and Justice** page 32).

508 altars and seats of the gods are nowhere to be seen This is the very sacrilege that Clytaemnestra has warned against (324–5). Coming so soon after the Chorus' concerns about the possible repercussions of Agamemnon's success (357, 443–4, 450–6), the herald's statement is ominous.

Legal imagery

513–18 The herald uses the language of court cases (see **Legal imagery** page 6) handling theft and consequent compensation. Paris and Troy are equally guilty (Paris for abducting Helen, Troy for harbouring them both) and they are therefore equally liable (513) for the debt owed to the Greeks. Once convicted of theft, the guilty have to pay double compensation (518): the value of what has been stolen and the same amount again. Thus those of Priam's sons that have not already paid with their lives must both return Helen and endure the destruction of Troy (516–17).

Stichomythia

519–31 The Chorus reveal to the herald that all is not well in Argos: the herald's assumption that the homecoming is the beginning of a happy ending to the Trojan War is dashed.
- Consider the structure of these lines and the way in which the dialogue moves from the herald's profession that he could now die happy (520) to that of the Chorus (531). Why is *stichomythia* an effective form for these few lines (see *Stichomythia* page 26)?
- Do you imagine this is the welcome home the herald expected?
○ Consider his appearance: might he look smart or ragged?

You had your fill of hostility by Scamander's banks,
But now, be a saviour and healer,
Lord Apollo; and I address all the gods
Of the assembly, and my patron   495
Hermes, kind herald, by heralds revered,
And the heroes who sent us out: welcome back
Favourably those troops spared by the spear.
Hail, royal halls, dear house,
Holy seats and gods who face the sun,   500
If ever you have before, give the king proper welcome now
After his long absence with your eyes shining;
For he is coming and brings light in the darkness for you
And for all these here to share in – our lord Agamemnon.
Give a good welcome, as is indeed right,   505
To the man who demolished Troy with the mattock
Of Zeus that brings justice – with it he levelled her plains:
The altars and seats of the gods are nowhere to be seen
And the seed of the whole land has been exterminated.
Such is the yoke he threw on Troy –   510
Lord Atreides, august, a man blessed by fortune –
And he is coming, of men alive the most deserving of honour;
For neither Paris nor Troy – and both must pay –
Can boast that his deed was greater than their suffering.
Judged guilty of robbery and rape, Paris lost   515
What he had stolen and he cut down his father's house
To its roots, destroying it utterly:
The sons of Priam have paid double compensation.

CHORUS Herald from the army of the Achaeans, hail.
HERALD Hail to you; no more will I begrudge the gods my death.   520
CHORUS Was it love for your native land that wore you down?
HERALD So much so that my eyes are starting to weep for joy.
CHORUS Timely, then, was the sickness that oppressed you.
HERALD How so? Tell me that I may master your meaning.
CHORUS Those you yearned for in your affliction longed for you.   525
HERALD Then this land longed for the army, itself full of longing?
CHORUS Yes. How often my low spirits made me sigh.

Physical hardships

536 Were I to speak of hardship   The herald describes the hardships endured by the ordinary Greek soldiers on the voyage out to Troy and during the long siege (536–48). Such details are absent from the Homeric account: in the *Iliad* the focus is on the interaction between the heroes, on and off the battlefield, rather than the harsh conditions endured by the rank and file.

545 Ida   is a mountain near Troy (see note on 267).

559 nailed up these spoils in the halls   The phrase is formulaic. The victor hangs his spoils (items of weaponry or armour) on the wall of the temple as a dedication, both to record his success and thank the gods for it.

562 Zeus' benevolence   As in his first speech, the herald pays respect to the gods (490–6) and acknowledges that events take place in accordance with Zeus' will (see **Zeus and Justice** page 32): the same view appears in the opening lines of the *Iliad*.

The Herald tells of his experiences at Troy. Scene from the National Theatre production, London, 1981.

HERALD Why this gloomy anxiety about the army?

CHORUS Silence has long been my antidote to harm.

HERALD What? Was there one you feared with the rulers away? 530

CHORUS So much that, as you said, I could happily die now.

HERALD Yes, things have worked out well; though with time
People may claim that our luck was not absolute,
That we had much to complain about too; who except the gods
Goes through a whole lifetime without suffering? 535
Were I to speak of hardship and rough quarters,
Of narrow gangways and hard bed-mats – what did we not
Groan about, what were we not dealt as our daily lot?
And then on dry land, the torment was even greater:
Our beds were right by the walls of the enemy, 540
And the dew from the heavens
And from the meadows soaked us through, a continual scourge,
Infesting our woollen clothes with lice.
I could speak of the winters that killed the birds,
The intolerable sufferings brought by the snows of Ida, 545
Or the heat, when the waves of the sea fell
And slept in their windless noonday bed;
What need is there to grieve over all that? The struggle is over,
It is over, and not even those who died
Would care ever to rise again; 550
For those of us who are left of the Argive army, what we have gained
Matters most: no suffering outweighs that.
Why count how many lives were wasted,
Why should the living suffer for others' malignant ill-fortune?
It is right, I think, to bid a firm farewell to bad times 555
And proper to boast to this day's sun,
As we wing our way over land and sea:
'Having taken Troy at last, the Argive expedition
Has nailed up these spoils in the halls
Of the gods throughout Greece to abide in splendour.' 560
Everyone who hears this news should glorify the city
And her generals; and Zeus' benevolence, which accomplished this,
Shall be honoured. You have the whole story.

Irony

568 I cried out for joy The fifth-century audience would be familiar with Homer's account of Agamemnon's homecoming (see *Background to the story*) in which Clytaemnestra was not renowned for her loyalty to her husband during his absence at Troy (unlike Penelope in the *Odyssey*). They would therefore be sensitive to the possible irony here – in Clytaemnestra's cry for joy (note on 28) – and later (481, 581–2, 830–1, 859, 883, 946).

Male and female

573 How very like a woman Whether Clytaemnestra is referring to the Chorus' specific aspersions (465–9, **Glory** page 40) or not, her credibility has been doubted because she is a woman (see **Male and female** pages 2 and 30). Now she has been vindicated, she gets some measure of revenge by describing the men's shouts of celebration (see note on 28) as those of women.

577–8 they piled on/The incense The people throw incense on the fire as an offering to the gods (see **Sacrifice** page 22): this has the effect of dousing the flames (see note on 95).

586 the city's sweetheart is an unexpected phrase for Clytaemnestra to use to address Agamemnon – especially if he is in fact unpopular (433–4) – when she is in the midst of emphasising how he is *her* sweetheart (581, 583, 588).

- Why might Clytaemnestra choose to use such a phrase?

588 a noble watchdog Clytaemnestra's phrase might recall to the audience the same word used by the watchman of himself (3).

- In what respect is Clytaemnestra a similar 'watchdog' to the watchman? Is there any irony (see **Irony** above) in her use of the word?

591 No seal broken Clytaemnestra refers primarily to the habit of sealing the storage jars, and thus the wealth of the house, while its master is away, but there is innuendo here, implying fidelity to Agamemnon during his absence.

Clytaemnestra's speech (568–95)

Clytaemnestra speaks in public about private matters; she parades her wifely devotion (580–95); she finishes with a claim to know what is expected of a woman, despite her tendency to embody what are seen as male characteristics (10–11, 337). She vows she has adhered to that expectation. The Chorus warn the herald not to take her speech at face value (597).

- What does Clytaemnestra say that may be 'open to sharp interpretation' (597) by the herald or the audience (see **Irony** above)?
- What impression is Clytaemnestra wanting to create by her speech?
- What does this speech add to the understanding of her character?

CHORUS I am happy to be won over by your words:
Even in old men the desire to learn is ever fresh.   565
Such news will naturally be of most interest to Clytaemnestra
And this house; but it makes me rich too.

CLYTAEMNESTRA I cried out for joy long before now,
When the first messenger of fire arrived in the night
And told of the capture and destruction of Ilium;   570
And people criticised me, saying: 'Is it the fire-signals that
Induce you to think that Troy has now been sacked?
How very like a woman to have her spirits raised.'
Such talk made me look muddled;
Even so I kept making the sacrifices, and up and down   575
Throughout the city like women they began to shriek cries of joy,
Shouting in triumph; and in the homes of the gods they piled on
The incense, lulling the flames that consumed the sacrifice.
And now what need for you to tell me anything more?
I will learn the whole story from my lord himself;   580
I will rush to greet my honoured husband
In the best possible way when he comes back; for what
Day could be sweeter for a wife to see than when
She opens the gates to her husband brought back safe by a god
From campaign? Take these words back to my husband: 585
Come as quickly as possible – the city's sweetheart;
And when he gets here, let him find in his home
As faithful a wife as the one he left behind, a noble watchdog
Over the halls on his behalf, foe to those who wished him ill,
Unchanged in all other respects too,   590
No seal broken over the course of time; I know
Neither pleasure from another man nor disapproving comment
Any more that I know how to temper bronze.
Such is my boast, full of truth,
No disgrace for a noble woman to make.   595

Clytaemnestra's departure

596 This woman has spoken Clytaemnestra asks the herald to take a message to Agamemnon (585–93). It seems natural that she then leaves the stage at the end of her speech; if she does remain on stage (see **A silent presence** page 12), the Chorus speak boldly (597) in her presence.

● If Clytaemnestra does not leave the stage at this point (595), would her presence be significant for anything that is said in the rest of this episode (596–661)?

599 dear ruler of this land Menelaus is king of Sparta, but the Chorus speak as if he rules Argos (see notes on 3 and 384). The satyr play (see *Introduction to the Greek Theatre*) performed on the same day as the *Oresteia* trilogy and also written by Aeschylus, dealt with Menelaus' adventures in Egypt, where he is shipwrecked after the storm that the herald describes; the play has not survived.

614 Helios The Greek word for the sun and therefore also used to personify it in divine form. The sun conventionally sees all things.

617 pollute an auspicious day It is a bad omen either to utter or to hear bad news on a day of celebration, and the herald is therefore reluctant to tell the story of Menelaus' disappearance on a day which should be bringing happiness to Argos (628).

623 double scourge War brings misery both for the city as a whole and for the individual household (421–31).

626 sing the dark Furies' holy hymn The holy hymn (*paean*) is a song of happy celebration and healing appropriate to Apollo the Healer (see **Apollo the Healer** page 16); that the Furies would have a *paean* is an oxymoron.

CHORUS This woman has spoken and now you know –
A fine-sounding speech, but open to sharp interpretation.
Now, herald, speak out – I seek news of Menelaus,
If the dear ruler of this land has returned safe with you
And is due to reach his home.   600

HERALD I cannot tell fine lies
For my friends to feed off for long.

CHORUS Then your news cannot be true *and* good?
When they diverge, it is not easy to hide the fact.

HERALD He has disappeared from the Achaean fleet.   605
Both he and his ship: that is the truth.

CHORUS In full view as he put out to sea from Ilium?
Or did a storm afflict you all and snatch him from the army?

HERALD Like a champion archer, you have hit the mark,
Neatly summing up this great loss.   610

CHORUS Is there any talk of him among the sailors –
Whether he is alive or dead?

HERALD Nobody knows or can say for sure
Except Helios who sustains life on earth.

CHORUS Tell us then, how did the storm hit the army of ships?   615
Were the gods angry? And how did it end?

HERALD It is not right to pollute an auspicious day
By reporting bad news; keep worship free of it.
When a messenger, with grim expression,
Brings the bad news a city prayed never to hear, its army defeated,   620
A single common wound for all its people striking the city;
Many homes purged of many men
By the double scourge that Ares loves,
A two-pronged destruction, bloodily yoked –
When one is burdened with grief like that,   625
Then is the right time to sing the dark Furies' holy hymn;
But when the good news that safety is assured
Arrives in a city rejoicing in prosperity –
How can I mix good with bad by describing
The storm and the anger of the gods against the Achaeans?   630
Fire and water – deadly enemies before –
Conspired together and proved their pact
By destroying the wretched army of the Argives.

635 Winds from Thrace Winds from the north bring trouble (178–83, 1390).

Rustic imagery

638 some terrible shepherd The ships are like sheep which are frightened by a malicious shepherd; the herald uses several images taken from country life (506, 636, 640, 650): his use of such imagery helps to shape his character.

Legal imagery

643 won us a reprieve Another piece of legal imagery (see **Legal imagery** page 6): in court a speaker can win a reprieve by clever pleading. The herald imagines that 'some god' has pleaded the case for his ship in some hypothetical divine court and won it a reprieve from destruction; as a consequence, Fortune takes over the tiller of his ship (645) and guides it to safety. The term 'deliverer' (*sōtēr*) is commonly used of Zeus (see **A thank-offering to Zeus** page 102).

656 You should confidently expect

● Has the herald given any justification for such confidence?

659 destroy his line utterly Menelaus has no son and now he has disappeared: such calamity leads the herald to the possibility that Zeus wants Menelaus' line to be extinguished.

Second Episode (484–661)

● What does the herald say that helps to make him sympathetic?
● Is he a religious man?
● What is the cumulative effect of his gloomy picture of the Greek experience at Troy?
● What does the herald say about Agamemnon?
● Does the scene advance the action of the play?

Terrible waves rose up in the night:
Winds from Thrace dashed the ships against 635
One another, some violently rammed by others in the storm
Of the hurricane and its rain-drumming deluge – they were
Out of sight and gone, in the swirl of some terrible shepherd.
When the shining light of the sun returned,
We saw the Aegean sea flowering with the corpses 640
Of the men of Achaea and the wreck of their ships;
But as for us and our ship with its hull still intact,
Someone smuggled us away or won us a reprieve,
Not a man, but some god, his hand on the tiller.
Fortune the deliverer graciously took her seat in our ship, 645
And so it was not swamped by the swell while at anchor
Nor run aground on the rocky shoreline.
Finally, not believing our luck in escaping
A watery death, in the glare of the daylight
We let our thoughts graze over our recent sufferings, 650
The exhausted army still in torment.
Even so, if any of the others are alive,
They will be saying that we are dead – why wouldn't they? –
And we assume the same is true of them.
But may all turn out for the best. So, first 655
You should confidently expect Menelaus to return;
And then, if a ray of sun does find him
Living and breathing – and Zeus' design
Is not to destroy his line utterly –
There is some hope he will again reach his home. 660
All that you have just heard is true: be sure of it.

SECOND CHORAL ODE (2ND *STASIMON*) (662–756)

The focus of the First Stasimon was the consequences of Helen's abduction for the Greeks; the focus of the Second Stasimon is its consequences for the Trojans. In the first part of this stasimon (662–725) the Chorus picture the arrival of Helen at Troy and reflect on its repercussions; in the second part (726–56) they consider why men commit wicked and arrogant acts.

662 gave her this name   The Greek root *hel-* means 'destruction' or 'capture', lending itself to a consequent pun (669). The Chorus marvel at the suitability of Helen's name in the light of 'what lay fated ahead' (665): the eventual destruction of Troy.

667 spear for her groom   Helen brings war both to her previous husband (Menelaus) and to her new one (Paris).

672 the Giant Zephyr   The wind that blows from the west and which would have driven Paris' ship with Helen back to Troy. Zephyr is a child of the immortal Titans and all their children are Giants. The 'many shield-bearing men' (673) are the Greeks, tracking Helen and Paris across the sea to Troy along the same route they took.

676 Simois   A river near Troy.

Impersonal forces

677 Strife   The Chorus have previously imagined that Zeus sent a Fury (see **The Furies** page 8) in the form of the Atreidae to punish the Trojans (55–62) and has thrown a net of destruction over Troy (341–7). Now they imagine a Trojan War orchestrated by the impersonal forces (see **Impersonal forces** page 34) Strife (*Eris* 677) and Wrath (*Menis* 679), the last named angry at Paris' betrayal of Menelaus' hospitality: 'wrath' (*mēnis*) is the first word of the *Iliad*, establishing the theme of that poem.

678–9 wedlock –/A term well named   The Greek *kēdos* (wedlock) means both a bond by marriage and grief or trouble: Helen is both for the Trojans.

The hearth

682–3 dishonoured both table/And Zeus of the hearth   The hearth (*hestia*) is the fireplace and focal point of the Greek home, its fire providing a source of heat and light. The fire in the hearth often comes to symbolise the well-being of the house itself (see **The house** page 2). The hearth also symbolises the hospitality of a house: after a ten-year delay ('though late', 681) Paris pays for his breach of it (see **Hospitality** page 8).

CHORUS   Who was it who gave her this name,
              True in every respect,
            If not one whom we cannot see;
              Knowing what lay fated ahead,   665
              He cleverly named her Helen,
          A spear for her groom, a conflict for many,
                A name that was apt:
          Hell on ships, hell for men, hell in cities,
                She sailed away from   670
              Her bed-drapes of luxury
            On the breeze of the Giant Zephyr,
          And many shield-bearing men, hunters
              Along the invisible trail of oars,
                Came to the shores   675
                Of leafy Simois –
            The work of blood-soaked Strife.

          Wrath forced Ilium into a wedlock –
            A term well named – Wrath who
                Accomplishes her will;   680
          She exacted her vengeance, though late,
          On those who dishonoured both table
                And Zeus of the hearth,
              On those who heartily sang
            The bridal song which on that day   685
          It befell the bridegroom's kin to sing.
          But then, learning a different song,
              The aged city of Priam
          Wails out a loud cry of mourning, calling
              Paris 'the murderous groom'.   690
              Troy has endured a time
              Full of destruction and grief
        At the pitiful shedding of her citizens' blood.

A lion cub

695 The cub of a lion   The Chorus supplement their account (662–93) of the consequences of Helen's abduction for the Trojans by comparing her to a lion cub (694–724). The lion is the symbol of the house of Atreus (see **The mauling of Troy** page 62, note on 1194–5); as a female member of the house (**The house** page 2), Helen is like a cub – just as she was the young of the vultures (see note on 49–54) – kept indoors and protected. The lion cub (Helen) is brought into a man's home (Troy) and pampered as a new pet (697–703). However, with time the cub grows up and reveals its true nature (704–5), causing carnage in the house (707–11); so with time Helen reveals herself (666–9) for what she is – the cause of misery and carnage for the Trojans. The Chorus call the cub a 'priest of Destruction' (712). The metaphor can also be applied to the situation of Helen and Menelaus. By marrying her and giving her a home, Menelaus in effect 'raises' (694) Helen, but she turns on her 'guardians' (706) and reveals her destructive nature, by eloping with Paris and thus causing the deaths of many Greeks who went to reclaim her.

703 Fawning from its belly's needs   The lion cub pretends to be playful in order to be given food.

707–8 a feast …/From the carnage   What begins as a sacrifice of sheep quickly shifts to a massacre of humans (711).

Helen

714 there came to the city of Ilium   The Chorus end their account (714–25) with further metaphorical language: Helen is a 'delicate jewel' (717) when she arrives at Ilium with her air of calm (715–16). In time, however, her marriage to Paris proves fatal to the Trojans (722) and turns out to be a Fury sent by Zeus (723), punishing both the Trojans and Helen herself (725). In the *Iliad* (*iii*, 171–6; *vi*, 344–53; *xxiv*, 764) Helen is often found lamenting the fact that she caused the Trojan War and wishing she were dead.

Just so did a man raise in his home
The cub of a lion, craving the breast   695
    But starved of milk;
    At the start of its life
    Gentle, friendly to children
    And a joy to old men;
Many a thing did it clutch in its arms   700
    Like some child new born,
Its beaming face fixed on the hand and
    Fawning from its belly's needs.

In time it revealed the traits
    It took from its parents: 705
It repaid its guardians for their kindness
By preparing a feast, though unbidden,
From the carnage of slaughtered sheep,
And the house was defiled with blood:
Overpowering anguish for the household,   710
    The great scourge of a massacre.
A priest of Destruction had been raised
    In the house by a god.

At first there came to the city of Ilium
    What I would call a spirit   715
    Of unruffled serenity,
    A delicate jewel of opulence,
    A soft shot from the eyes,
A blossoming of love to gnaw at the heart.
But the marriage was knocked off course   720
    And brought to a bitter end.
Fatal to the house, fatal to its company,
    Sent by Zeus, lord of hospitality,
There pounced on the children of Priam
    A Fury to make a bride weep.   725

The Chorus reflect (726–56)

*In the last part of the First Stasimon, the Chorus ended with some reflection on the 'moral' of the story, rejecting fame and success because they cause resentment (see **Resentment** page 40). In the last part of this Second Stasimon, the Chorus end with some reflection on the cause of wickedness and their 'moral' is that Justice will honour the righteous man (750).*

The cause of wickedness

726 An old saying was fashioned The Chorus consider (726–47) why men commit wicked or arrogant acts. They reject (732) the common view that it is great success and prosperity that lead to arrogant acts (726–9); they believe that only those with an arrogant or wicked nature will commit arrogant or wicked acts (733–5, 741–3). They employ metaphorical language when expressing this belief: arrogance (*hubris*) breeds (729) or gives birth (742) to arrogance, the offspring resembles its parents (747). The Chorus are sure that those without a wicked nature (736) will not commit wicked acts – their 'children' will be 'fine' (737). The connection to the first part of the *stasimon* may be that Paris' wicked act – his abduction of Helen – has its roots in an earlier crime (see below), but the Chorus do not explicitly say so; they do observe that an arrogant act brings destruction on the house (745–6), which is unquestionably true of Paris' act (516–17).

Agamemnon's inherited guilt

735 Children in its own image The Chorus' thoughts (726–47) may equally, but less explicitly, refer to Agamemnon. Their suggestion is that guilt is inherited from parents (731): children will have to pay for their parents' sins, arrogance breeds arrogance (741–3).
Agamemnon's father Atreus perpetrated an act of wickedness (see *Background to the story*); the implication must be that this led to Agamemnon's own wicked act – the sacrifice of Iphigeneia – which will in turn (see **A second cycle of vengeance** page 98) lead to one perpetrated by his son (see **Orestes** page 66).

Daimōn

744 a *daimōn* invincible A *daimōn* is a powerful spirit (see note on 370) that attaches itself to an individual, often to affect his fortune adversely. An act of wickedness can call up a *daimōn*, which then plagues the wicked man and possibly his family or house (see **The house** page 2).

An old saying was fashioned, spoken long ago
Amongst men, that when a man's
Happiness reaches great heights,
It does not die without issue, but breeds –
His prosperity gives birth   730
To misery without end for his heirs.
I stand apart from the rest
And alone in my belief that it is the wicked act
That gives birth to more after it,
Children in its own image;   735
While it is always the fate of a law-abiding house
To have fine children.
Sooner or later
For all men who are wicked,
The day fixed for the birth will arrive;   740
Then age-old arrogance
Will give birth
To fresh arrogance
And to a *daimōn* invincible, irresistible –
Their unholy audacity   745
Will bring black destruction on their house:
Offspring that takes after its parents.

Optimism and pessimism

756 all things she directs to their end Once again (see **Optimism and pessimism** page 14) the Chorus' outlook is both optimistic and pessimistic, though this time less explicitly. They hold the optimistic belief that Justice honours the righteous man, even if he is poor, and abandons the unclean man, even if he is wealthy (748–55). However, this belief becomes pessimistic if applied to Agamemnon, who is wealthy and acclaimed (754–5) but whose hands are horribly unclean from the sacrifice of his daughter (see **Sacrifice** page 22). The *stasimon* thus finishes – and Agamemnon now arrives – on an ominous note.

● Is this why the Chorus make no reference in the *stasimon* to Agamemnon's imminent return?

THIRD EPISODE (757–947)

*Agamemnon returns triumphant in a chariot (879) to Argos, having sacked Troy (see **Passing of time** page 42); he is accompanied by Cassandra, his prize from Troy, and possibly some attendants. He greets his native land and the Chorus; Clytaemnestra then explains how his absence affected her. A rich cloth is laid out for him to walk on and he goes into the palace.*

○ Consider how you might stage such an important entrance. Should it be noisy or muted? What would Agamemnon be wearing? How many attendants might he have?

Moment of triumph

757 king, city-sacker of Troy Agamemnon is now at the height of his power and the peak of his success, yet the previous *stasimon* (see above) and the Chorus' earlier concerns (235–7, **The Chorus' concerns** page 38) have combined to create a tense, expectant atmosphere. Just as nowadays 'pride comes before a fall', so in ancient literature it is a common theme that a man must be on his guard all the more at the very peak of his success.

760 not to overdo and yet not understate The Chorus are wary of giving Agamemnon excessive praise (450–1) but they do want to give him due credit for sacking Troy.

Sincerity

763 set more store by pretence The Chorus – and later Agamemnon (812–14) – know that many men are willing to tell lies, whether to please or to deceive; they have already questioned Clytaemnestra's sincerity (597) and the herald confessed that he could not lie (601–2) even to cheer his friends. By being honest about what their feelings were when the expedition departed (773–5) and about the sacrifice of Iphigeneia (776–8), in their desperation the Chorus hope to persuade Agamemnon to listen to their warning now – not to trust everyone who seems to be well intentioned towards him (762–72).

But Justice glitters
Even in homes grimy with smoke
And honours the righteous man;   750
With eyes averted she abandons gilded palaces
And hands unclean and instead
She approaches the devout:
For she pays no honour to the power of wealth
Falsely hallmarked with acclaim;   755
And all things she directs to their end.

Come now, king, city-sacker of Troy,
Offspring of Atreus,
How shall I address you? How am I to honour you?
How not to overdo and yet not understate   760
The right measure of praise?
Once they overstep the mark of justice,
Many men set more store by pretence.
Everyone is ready to sigh for a man
Who is suffering, but the bite of sorrow   765
Does not reach right to their hearts;
And they join in another's rejoicing with copied expression,
Forcing a smile that's not there.

778 a sacrifice   The death of Iphigeneia.

783 who should not have   Men of military age were obliged to fight. Although no names are mentioned, the Chorus seem to have someone in mind.

An urgent warning
757–83   The Chorus have talked of their anxiety (99), reported Calchas' warning of a treacherous steward in the house (143) and the citizens' anger (439), and expressed the dangers of excess and injustice; now at the very moment of their king's return, they are more desperate to offer a warning than their congratulations.

- What may Agamemnon understand by the Chorus' first speech to him?
- Might the Chorus voice their concern openly because Clytaemnestra is not on stage (see **A silent presence** page 66)?
○ Would Agamemnon display any surprise at so anxious a welcome?

785 they share responsibility with me   Agamemnon thinks it right to share the credit for his success with the gods. In Sophocles' *Ajax*, Ajax denies needing the gods' help and is punished for his arrogance.

Legal imagery
789 cast their votes   Agamemnon imagines that the gods unanimously vote for Troy's destruction. The image is from the Athenian legal system (see **Legal imagery** page 6): each member of the jury drops his vote into one of two urns, one representing acquittal, the other condemnation. The juror passed his hands over both urns in order to keep his vote secret.

799 the Horse   The Wooden Horse, 'pregnant' with the Greek soldiers who entered Troy.

800 the Pleiades   A group of stars which set in winter: this is at odds with the tradition that Troy was sacked in the summer.

The mauling of Troy
801 flesh-eating lion   The lion is associated with the royal family of Argos (see note on 1194–5). The 'royal blood' is Trojan, for many of the Trojan royal family died (802) during the sack of Troy, including Priam, who was killed while seeking sanctuary at Zeus' altar.

- Does the wording of Agamemnon's description suggest he relishes Troy's destruction?

But whoever is a good judge of his flock
Will not fail to read the eyes of the man   770
Who fawns in watery friendship
With a show of well-meaning intent.
When you were gathering the army
For Helen's sake, I must admit to
Painting you in a terrible light;   775
You steered your thoughts off course too,
When you restored the spirits of starving men
By means of a sacrifice;
But now straight from the heart in all goodwill
I wish you well, now you have ended your labours successfully.   780
After long and careful questioning you will learn
Which citizens stayed at home in our city
With just cause – and who should not have.

AGAMEMNON   First Argos and its native gods
Do I greet, with justice: they share responsibility with me   785
For my homecoming and for the justice I exacted from
The city of Priam. The gods paid heed to appeals for justice
That were not couched in words; and without hesitation
They cast their votes, murderous and fatal for Ilium,
Into the urn of blood. At the opposite urn,   790
Destined to stay empty, only the hope of a hand drew near.
The city's capture is obvious even now from the smoke.
The whirlwind of destruction lives on; dying in its midst
Are the embers that send up plumes thick with wealth.
For this we must be mindful to pay repeated thanks to the gods,   795
Since we have taken inordinate plunder.
The beast of Argos has ground the city into dust
For the sake of a woman.
The offspring of the Horse, a shield-bearing troop,
Sprang forward in a bound at the setting of the Pleiades;   800
The flesh-eating lion leapt over the towers
And licked its fill of royal blood.

804 your observations   Agamemnon refers to what the Chorus have said (781–3) about how the citizens have acted in his absence.

807 not resent him   See **Resentment** page 40.

Sincerity

813 mirror of companionship   This image encompasses two ideas: first, that Agamemnon's companions merely reflect his feelings in order to please him (see **Sincerity** page 60); secondly, that – as reflections – these feelings are not genuine and have no substance. This may be a subtle allusion to Achilles, who seemed at first to be Agamemnon's ally, but then quarrelled with him and withdrew from the fighting at Troy (*Iliad i*); or it may be an allusion to Ajax, who tried to kill Agamemnon when Odysseus, not he, had been awarded the dead Achilles' armour (as told in Sophocles' *Ajax*) as a prize.

Odysseus

815–17   When Agamemnon was recruiting the Greek army, Odysseus was reluctant to leave his wife and new-born son Telemachus. He pretended to be mad by yoking an ass and an ox to his plough and sowing salt, but Agamemnon's envoys placed Telemachus in the path of the plough. When Odysseus turned the plough aside to avoid him, they knew his madness was a pretence.

816 Once yoked was a willing trace-horse   The image is of the outside horse in the chariot race. The two central yoke-horses pull a little harder on the straight as they are closer to the yoke, but on the bend the trace-horse is required to add extra effort to ensure a successful turn; hence a trace-horse comes to signify additional impetus at a crucial moment, here perhaps an allusion to the success of the Wooden Horse, which was Odysseus' idea. Agamemnon praises Odysseus' ability to work as part of a team, though by saying 'for me' Agamemnon implies that he himself was not part of that team, but the driver.

819 in full assembly   Agamemnon is king of Argos and power rests with him, but here he shows a willingness to listen to the advice of his council of elders and noblemen (495).

Agamemnon's speech (784–828)
- Consider the language that Agamemnon uses. What impression does he make? Does he speak like a king and successful commander?
- What are his attitudes to the war, the victory and the matters of state that await him? How does he respond to the Chorus' warnings?
- How important does it seem to be to Agamemnon to establish that his cause was just?

I have drawn out these opening remarks to the gods;
But as for your observations, I have heard them
And I bear them in mind; I agree with you   805
And you may count me your ally. It is in few men's nature
To respect a successful friend but not resent him.
A malignant poison settles in the heart and
Doubles the burden of one already plagued by suffering;
Such a person is oppressed by his own troubles   810
But also groans when he sees another's happiness.
I speak from knowledge, for well I understand
The mirror of companionship, an image of a shadow,
Men who appeared most well disposed towards me.
Only Odysseus, the man who refused to sail,   815
Once yoked was a willing trace-horse for me –
Whether the man I speak of be alive or dead.

But as for state and religious matters,
When all are gathered together in full assembly
We will hold talks. Whatever is going well –   820
We must discuss how it may continue so.
But wherever there is a call for healing medicine
Or cauterising-irons or amputation, we will try to be considerate
As we dispel the pain of infection.
Now I shall go into my house, my hearth and home,   825
And first I shall salute the gods,
Those who sent me out and brought me back.
May the success that attends me hold firm.

A silent presence

829 Men of the city   Once again (see **A silent presence** page 12) it is not certain whether Clytaemnestra has been on stage for part of a scene.

○ If Clytaemnestra was present for Agamemnon's homecoming speech, how might his failure to address her be highlighted? Though he does not speak to her, might he greet her in some other way? Might she be content to remain in the background?

○ If she was not present for the speech, when might be a significant time for her to enter? Might she come out of the palace to stop Agamemnon going inside? What might he make of her not coming out of the palace as soon as he arrived?

844 Geryon   A half-human monster with three heads and three torsos: Hercules kills him and steals his cattle as one of his labours.

Clytaemnestra's imagery

845 coat of earth   An unusual way to describe burial.

● Why might Clytaemnestra dwell on the reports of Agamemnon's death (840–6)? What might be the effect of the content and language of this passage on Agamemnon himself?

850 That is why our child   Although it quickly becomes clear (852) that these words refer to the missing Orestes (see below), their meaning is initially ambiguous, since they could equally refer to Iphigeneia. This is the first time in her speech that Clytaemnestra speaks directly to Agamemnon – and this scene is the first time that they have seen each other since the death of Iphigeneia. In the *Odyssey* Agamemnon tells Odysseus that he had expected a joyful welcome from his children (see *Background to the story*).

● Why might Clytaemnestra wish to be ambiguous?

Orestes

852 Orestes   Clytaemnestra and Agamemnon's son. She has to explain his absence, since Agamemnon would expect him to be present in Argos. She has sent him to Strophius (854), who is Orestes' uncle. Phocis is some distance from Argos; the family connection might make it a good choice in Agamemnon's eyes, the location in Clytaemnestra's. Orestes is the central character of the *Choephoroi* and the defendant on trial in the *Eumenides*, the second and third plays respectively in the *Oresteia* trilogy (see **The story continues** page 120).

853 spear-friend   An ally of war, bound by mutual ties of loyalty and obliged to come to one's aid or defence if needed.

CLYTAEMNESTRA Men of the city, you elders of Argos,
    I am not ashamed to tell you   830
    My feelings of love for my husband; with time people's timidity
    Dies away. Not from others
    Have I learned this, I speak of my own life, miserable
    All the while this man was at Ilium.
    First, for a woman to sit abandoned at home   835
    Away from her husband is a terrible evil.
    She hears many festering rumours:
    One person comes, then another, bringing
    Worse news after bad, crying it out to the house.
    If this man here had met with as many wounds   840
    As reports that poured into this home, you would say
    A net had fewer holes than he had drilled into him.
    If he had died as many times as the rumours multiplied,
    He would have needed three bodies – a second Geryon –
    And have boasted that he donned a coat of earth   845
    Three times, dying once for each body.
    Such festering rumours meant that
    Many times, while gripping me hard,
    They freed my neck from a noose high above.
    That is why our child, guardian of your and my promises,   850
    Does not stand here as would be right –
    Orestes. Do not be surprised at this.
    Our loyal spear-friend is looking after him:
    Strophius the Phocian, since he warned me of
    Twofold troubles: the danger for you there at Troy   855
    And the lawless clamour of our people here, which might
    Topple the council, since it is the nature
    Of mortals to kick a man harder when he is down.

Orestes' absence

859 conceals no trickery   Clytaemnestra is at pains to stress the sincerity (see **Sincerity** pages 60 and 64) of her explanation for Orestes' absence.

- Does she produce a convincing explanation for Orestes' absence?
- Does her reference to unrest (856) suggest she did hear (see **A silent presence** page 66) the Chorus (see note on 757–83) and Agamemnon (819–24)? Or might she be trying to flatter Agamemnon that his absence made Argos less secure (856–7)?
- What is so significant about the content of this passage (850–67), that Clytaemnestra should address Agamemnon directly, whereas in the rest of the speech she refers to him in the third person?

Praise of Agamemnon

869 I may say that   Clytaemnestra now employs no fewer than seven images (869–74) to illustrate her relief that Agamemnon is home.

- What is the effect of such effusive praise?

870 fore-stay   A cable that runs from the mast to the front (fore) of the deck and, together with other cables (stays) attached to the mast, keeps it securely in place when the ship is under full sail.

The cloth

882 Spread the cloth   The appearance of the cloth, together with Agamemnon's arrival, make this the most striking scene visually in the play. The cloth cost a great deal (922), is coloured with expensive purple dye (933) and is worthy of being used to honour the gods (895) – a man should therefore be afraid to walk on it (882 and note on 930). Because purple was expensive (see note on 920), it symbolises royalty; it may also suggest the colour of blood.

- What is the symbolism of the purple cloth? How can it be most effectively exploited?
- In which direction might the cloth be laid out? From the palace to the chariot or vice versa? Or starting between the two and laid out in both directions? Consider the symbolism of each option.

884 for Justice to lead him down   Clytaemnestra, like Agamemnon before her (785–7), is sure that Justice is on her side.

Truly – this explanation conceals no trickery.
As for me, the gushing springs of my tears 860
Have dried up: there is not one drop left.
In my eyes I still bear the pain of late watches,
As I wept that the fire-beacons set for you
Were ever untouched. I used to be woken
From my dreams by the slightest whirring 865
Of a buzzing gnat; I saw suffering surround you,
More suffering than was possible in the time I slept.
After enduring all this, with a mind now free from grief
I may say that this man is a watchdog to the fold,
A saving fore-stay to the ship, to the high roof 870
A foundation post, an only child to its father,
Land appearing to sailors beyond their hopes,
A dawn most beautiful to behold after a storm,
A flowing stream to the thirsting traveller.
Yes, release from dire need is always sweet. 875
I think it right to address him in this way.
There must be no resentment here, for we have already suffered
Too many troubles. So now, my dear love,
Dismount from this chariot, but do not touch the ground,
My lord, with the foot that trampled Troy. 880
Servant women! Why the delay? You have your orders:
Spread the cloth on the ground for him to walk on.
Let his way into a home he never hoped to see
Be quickly laid out in purple, for Justice to lead him down.

Clytaemnestra's speech (829–86)

Agamemnon did not mention his wife or any other personal matters in his speech – he was concerned with men's business. Clytaemnestra portrays the war from the viewpoint of a loving, anxious wife and mother: it is a personal (833) account of the king's wife, left behind in a difficult predicament, and contains poignant detail (848–9, 860–7). She paints a vivid picture – as when describing (306–23) the sack of Troy – of the devoted wife waiting at home as news of her husband arrives; yet there is good reason to believe that she is describing experiences she has not necessarily had; clues in her speech suggest her words may not be sincere (see **Irony** page 48, **Clytaemnestra's imagery** page 66, notes on 859 and 869, and *Background to the story*).

- What sort of welcome does she give Agamemnon? Does she congratulate him on his success?
- Is her account of her suffering convincing? Does it fit the picture of Clytaemnestra that you have built up thus far in the play?
- How much irony can be found in her final lines (883–6)?
- Does she say anything which suggests she has heard (**A silent presence** page 66) Agamemnon's speech (784–828)?

887 Offspring of Leda   Zeus, in the guise of a swan, had an affair with the mortal Leda; she gave birth to two eggs: one contained the twins Castor and Polydeuces (who later became gods), the other Helen. Clytaemnestra was Leda's daughter by Tyndareus (see **A silent presence** page 12).

889 Protracted and lengthy

- Is this Agamemnon's attempt at a joke or a genuine criticism?

Barbarian excesses

891–2 do not pamper me...   First Agamemnon protests at being pampered like a woman; like the Chorus earlier (465–9), he too casts aspersions on female traits. He then explains that the barbarian habit of prostration before royalty is also abhorrent to him (893). He believes it would be typical of a foreign king like Priam to walk on valuable cloth (909). That would not fit the character of Priam as presented in the *Iliad*, who is in no way prone to excess; there the Trojans are no different from the Greeks in their customs or attitudes. Fifth-century Athenians (and Greeks) were proud to be free men, viewing barbarians as mere slaves of their king. Aeschylus himself fought in resistance to an attempted Persian invasion of Greece at Marathon in 490 BC; before *Agamemnon* he had written the *Persians*, which dealt with a later battle between Athenians and Persians at Salamis (480 BC) and was part of a trilogy that won first prize at the dramatic competition (see *Introduction to the Greek Theatre*).

As for the rest, the gods and my watchfulness, unconquered   885
By sleep, will with justice bring to pass what is fated.

AGAMEMNON Offspring of Leda, guardian of my halls,
You have spoken in a way that befits my absence:
Protracted and lengthy. However, it must be
For others to honour me with proper acclaim.   890
As for the rest, do not pamper me
Like a woman: do not gawp as if I were some barbarian fellow,
Shouting and prostrating yourself before me.

Agamemnon returns home in triumph. Scene from the
National Theatre production, London, 1981.

894 path to resentment Too much success incurs the resentment (*phthonos*) of the gods (see **Resentment** page 40). Agamemnon knows this and is careful to express his debt to the gods (784, 795–6, 826). He is also aware of the effect his success may have on his fellow men (807). He knows that his walking on the cloth would incur resentment (894–7, 919) and would be tantamount to equating himself to the gods (898).

901 A man should only be judged fortunate It is often noted in tragedy that one cannot be sure what the future holds; one must therefore reserve judgement whether a man is inherently fortunate until his life is over.

Agamemnon addresses Clytaemnestra (887–903)

- How affectionate are the first words Agamemnon addresses directly to his wife after his ten-year absence? What tone does he use towards her?
- How many of the points that she made in her speech does he answer? How sympathetic is he towards the suffering she has experienced?

Stichomythia (904–16)

904 Now tell me your thoughts Though Clytaemnestra has only a short while ago drawn attention to the danger of resentment (877), it now suits her to dismiss that danger (912). Agamemnon feels that walking on the cloth will mean that Clytaemnestra has defeated him (915), an argument she counters by a subtle paradox: he will maintain his authority by yielding (916). In this conflict of wills Clytaemnestra shows herself subtle in arguing and more than a match for her husband.

- How compelling are Clytaemnestra's arguments? Is she as persuasive as the Chorus have previously suggested (337–8, 597)?
- Is Agamemnon defeated by Clytaemnestra's arguments or his own weakness? Or does he change his mind to please her (917)?
- What is the dramatic effect of this sudden capitulation?
- With what gestures or actions might Clytaemnestra coax Agamemnon to walk on the cloth?

918 foot-servants on my travels

- Is the tone of this pun lighthearted (see note on 889)?

920 ocean-purple Garments are dyed purple using the juice of the murex shellfish, an expensive process, and therefore purple was the colour chosen by the rich and powerful.

921 great shame in damaging one's own property

- What were Agamemnon's earlier objections to walking on the cloth (895–8, 919)? What do they seem to be now?

Do not put me on a path to resentment by laying out
This cloth. Such material must be for honouring gods;   895
To my mind no mortal should walk
On such intricate handiwork unafraid.
What I am saying is: revere me as a man, not a god.
Fame speaks for itself without floor-coverings
Or fine handiwork, and good sense   900
Is god's greatest gift. A man should only be judged fortunate,
If he is still prospering when he reaches the end of his life.
If I manage all things like this, I am content.

CLYTAEMNESTRA Now tell me your thoughts honestly.

AGAMEMNON I will not hide what I think, be sure of that.   905

CLYTAEMNESTRA Might fear have made you vow it to the gods?

AGAMEMNON Yes, if some expert seer had declared it my duty.

CLYTAEMNESTRA What would Priam have done, had he won?

AGAMEMNON I am quite sure he would have walked on the cloth.

CLYTAEMNESTRA Then do not heed people's criticisms.   910

AGAMEMNON But what the people say carries great weight.

CLYTAEMNESTRA Only those with something to envy are resented.

AGAMEMNON A woman should not be so eager for a fight.

CLYTAEMNESTRA It is good for the victor to experience a defeat.

AGAMEMNON Does winning this argument mean so much to you?   915

CLYTAEMNESTRA Give in graciously! It confirms your authority.

AGAMEMNON If you think it right, then let someone quickly undo
My boots, foot-servants on my travels.
May no evil eye of resentment strike me from afar
As I tread on this ocean-purple fit for the gods.   920
There is great shame in damaging one's own property,
In destroying expensive cloth paid for in silver.

Cassandra

923–4 welcome in/This foreign girl Cassandra is the daughter of Priam and Hecuba, mentioned only once in Homer. Apollo loved her and gave her the gift of prophecy (see **Cassandra and Apollo** page 82). The Greek army voted to give Cassandra to Agamemnon as a sign of the esteem in which they hold him (927–8). Agamemnon does not disclose Cassandra's identity, but Clytaemnestra addresses her by name later (1006).

● What does the casual way in which Agamemnon introduces Cassandra to Clytaemnestra tell us about him?
● When Agamemnon tells Clytaemnestra to welcome Cassandra in, is he asserting his authority or just authoritative by nature?
○ How might you have Clytaemnestra react to Cassandra's presence when Agamemnon points her out?

929 since I am forced
● Is this a fair description of what happened (see *Stichomythia* page 72)?

930 trampling on this purple These words recall the Chorus' warning that the gods do care when a man tramples on the beauty of holy things (357).

● Agamemnon prepares to walk on the purple cloth, having effectively pronounced his own condemnation (895–8, 919). What effect does this have on the audience's sympathy for him?
● Why is it important for Clytaemnestra that he walk on the cloth?

937 the oracle's response Clytaemnestra claims that she consulted an oracle to find news of Agamemnon while he was at Troy, and to learn what rites she might perform to help ensure his return, which is so important to her (329, 938); it is common Greek practice to have recourse to oracles, prophets and other such agents of divination to learn about the future. The most famous oracle is that of Apollo at Delphi (see **Pythian Apollo** page 42).

940 the Dog Star's Sirius, which appears at the height of summer; see line 943: 'Zeus presses the wine' – the grapes are pressed in late summer.

Clytaemnestra's final speech

Clytaemnestra's praise of Agamemnon (869–74) was effusive, and she now uses contrary metaphors: warmth in winter (941–2) and coolness in summer (943–4). Her speech ends (as at 886) with words that appeal to the fulfilment of destiny, open to more than one interpretation (see **Irony** page 48).

● Why does the image of the house pervade Clytaemnestra's final speech?
● What is the effect of Clytaemnestra's using two opposing metaphors?
● What is Clytaemnestra's mood in her final speech (931–47)?

Well, so be it. Now, welcome in
This foreign girl graciously; god smiles from afar
On the master who is gentle;   925
No one willingly submits to the yoke of slavery.
This girl, a flower picked out from our horde of booty and
Given to me by the army, comes with me.
Now, since I am forced to heed you in this matter,
I will enter the halls of my house, trampling on this purple.   930
CLYTAEMNESTRA There is the sea – and who can drain that? –
Which nurtures an ever-fresh supply of purple,
Valuable as silver, used to dye cloth.
My lord, there is a good store of this under your roof, the gods
Be thanked: your house does not know what it means to be poor; 935
Indeed, I would have promised to trample a mass of cloth,
If this house had received such advice in the oracle's response
To me, as I looked for a way of saving this man's life.
As long as the roots still exist, foliage will come to the house and
Stretch its shade overhead against the Dog Star's heat.   940
So with your arrival at your hearth and home,
Warmth signals its arrival in winter,
And in the season when Zeus presses the wine
From the unripe grape, a coolness comes on the house
As its master moves through his home, fulfilling his role.   945
Zeus, Zeus, who brings fulfilment, fulfil my prayers:
Turn your mind now to what you will bring to fulfilment.

*Clytaemnestra
persuades
Agamemnon to walk
on the cloth. Scene
from the National
Theatre production,
London, 1981.*

Staging the Third Episode

o How prominent should the silent Cassandra be? What references to her presence are there?

o When should Agamemnon begin to walk on the cloth? When should he enter the palace? Should he hear Clytaemnestra's final exultant prayer (946–7)?

o At the end of the episode Clytaemnestra either follows Agamemnon into the palace (leaving Cassandra alone on stage with the Chorus and returning at 1005) or she and Cassandra both remain on stage during the ode. Explore both possibilities.

o If Clytaemnestra goes offstage now, does she take care to avoid walking on the cloth? What would you have happen to the cloth at the end of the episode?

o In staging the scene, what do you consider it most important to convey to the audience?

THIRD CHORAL ODE (3RD *STASIMON*) (948–1004)

The Chorus' fears (355–61) have been realised; without being specific as to its cause, they continue to express their concern (948–55), even though it has been a long time since the expedition left Aulis (956–60) and they have witnessed Agamemnon's safe return home themselves (961–2).

957–60 fastenings of the cables... These lines are obscure. Moored ships and the army setting out may refer to events at Aulis: the Chorus could be trying to calm their fears with the thought that Iphigeneia was sacrificed a long time ago. However, if these lines refer to the Trojan War as a whole, perhaps the Chorus recall the number of men killed in the war and worry that someone may be required to answer for those dead (443–4).

CHORUS   Why does this fear continue to hover
               Before my foreboding heart?
     It sings a song of prophecy, unpaid, unbidden;   950
       The confidence that used to reassure me
                Has left its seat
             And cannot persuade me
               To shrug this off
          Like an impenetrable dream.   955
            Time has now grown old
        Over the fastenings of the cables
          In the sand of the shore,
          Since the seafaring army
           Started against Ilium.   960

         With my own eyes I learn
    Of the army's return and witness it myself.
        Even so, my heart within me,
            Unprompted, chants
         A sombre dirge of the Furies.   965
         It holds not a single shred of
          The friendly cheer of hope.
          I feel it in my stomach
           When I think of justice;
          My heart is spun round   970
          In a whirl of fulfilment.
    Against all likelihood I pray it may prove
        False and without fulfilment.

Averting danger

974–92   The Chorus consider the dangers of disease and of wealth. Excessive wealth is dangerous, but its danger can be averted by disposing (978–85) of part of one's wealth – this way one's 'ship' (985) will not sink. Good health is never assured and disease can strike suddenly (974–7). The dangers of diseases caused by hunger can be averted by a good harvest (986–8). These solutions contrast with the fatal shedding of blood, for which there is no remedy (989–92).

Asclepius

994 the one man who well knew   Asclepius, Apollo's son, was such a good doctor that he could bring the dead back to life. Zeus, afraid that he might enable men to escape death altogether, killed him with a thunderbolt. He was worshipped throughout Greece; his most important sanctuary was at Epidaurus.

996 Had the gods not ordained   The gods have decreed that a man must not interfere in another man's destiny (996–8): the Chorus claim they would otherwise 'pour out their fears' (1000), perhaps meaning they would warn Agamemnon more specifically than they already have (762–83, note on 757–83).

The Chorus' fears (948–1004)

The *stasimon* is dominated by expressions of fear, but the Chorus do not explain why they are afraid.

- Is there any clue as to what makes them afraid?
- Why do you think that they do not refer to Agamemnon's walking on the cloth?
- What is the effect of this pessimistic (see **Optimism and pessimism** page 14) *stasimon,* coming so soon after the triumph (see **An urgent warning** page 62) of Agamemnon's return?

A man should be satisfied
To be in good health,   975
For disease is a neighbour
On the other side of the wall and pressing hard against it.
A man's destiny may hold a straight course,
But still crash on an unseen rock.
When caution with a well-measured throw   980
Empties overboard
Some part of a man's wealth,
Then his house does not groan and
Sink out of sight, sated by excess,
And his ship plumbs no depths.   985
So too, each year the ploughing leads
To generous and plentiful bounty from Zeus,
Putting an end to the diseases of hunger.

But once a man's
Dark and fatal blood   990
Falls onto the ground before him,
Who can recall it by the chanting of spells?
Zeus put a painful end
To the one man who well knew
How to bring back the dead.   995
Had the gods not ordained
That one man's fate
Should not encroach on another's,
My heart would have raced ahead of my tongue
To pour out these fears.   1000
But now it howls in the darkness,
Pained in spirit,
With no hope for a happy outcome,
While my mind is ablaze.

FOURTH EPISODE (1005–1301)

Clytaemnestra summons Cassandra inside (1005–16). The latter gives no indication that she hears or understands anything Clytaemnestra says, but starts to go into a state of trance preliminary to receiving a vision (1032–7); Clytaemnestra becomes impatient and goes back inside the palace (1038). Cassandra then undergoes a series of visions (1042–1143): she sees events from the troubled past of the palace (1061–8), then a new murder (1071–1100) and finally her own imminent death (1107–43). Because the Chorus are unable to follow her meaning, she describes her visions a second time (1149–1265) in more straightforward language. After a few final thoughts and predictions (1284–1301), she goes inside the palace.

1007 share in the purifications It is normal for slaves to participate in worship within the home: Clytaemnestra wants Cassandra to believe that she is entering a household where the normal rules apply (1016).

1008 the god of the household Zeus.

1010 Heracles The text has 'son of Alcmene'. The gods afflicted Heracles (*Hercules* is his Latin name) with illness as punishment for a murder he had committed, and he was then told by an oracle (see note on 937) that he could only be cured if he became a slave for three years. He was sold to Omphale, Queen of Lydia, and was forced to do woman's work for her.

● Are Clytaemnestra's words (1010–15) comforting or patronising?

1026 the central hearth A palace may have several hearths (see **The hearth** page 54); the central one is the most important and therefore most appropriate for a significant sacrifice (see **Sacrifice** page 22).

1031 *you* explain Clytaemnestra turns to the Chorus in exasperation.

1036–7 froth away her strength/In blood When being broken in, horses can exhaust themselves struggling against the bridle, which chafes the mouth and draws blood. The words 'bridle' (1037) and 'yoke' (1041) signify slavery.

Clytaemnestra's scene with Cassandra (1005–38)

1038 I will waste no more words Clytaemnestra leaves the stage. She may leave some attendants to watch over Cassandra.

● What parallels are there between Clytaemnestra's scene with Agamemnon and this scene with Cassandra?
● Why does Clytaemnestra fail to entice Cassandra into the palace?
● What is the tone of Clytaemnestra's remarks to Cassandra during this short scene? What does this tell us about Clytaemnestra's character?
● What role do the Chorus play in the scene?
○ Consider how Cassandra might act to warrant the description of her behaviour (1033, 1036).

CLYTAEMNESTRA You go inside too – I am talking to you,   1005
    Cassandra, since Zeus in his kindness has placed you in a home
    Where you can share in the purifications, standing among
    Our many slaves at the altar of the god of the household.
    Step out of the chariot and do not be proud.
    They say that once even Heracles   1010
    Suffered being sold and having to eat a slave's crust.
    If such misfortune must fall to one's lot,
    It is a great blessing to have masters with long-established wealth.
    Those who have reaped a good harvest beyond their hopes
    Are always harsh to their slaves.   1015
    So now you have heard me make the customary remarks.
CHORUS She was talking to you and her words were clear.
    Since you are trapped in the nets of destiny,
    Obey, if you are going to obey – but perhaps you will not obey.
CLYTAEMNESTRA Unless she is possessed   1020
    Of a strange tongue that no one understands, like some swallow,
    My words will have touched a nerve and persuaded her.
CHORUS Follow her in: as things stand, what she suggests is best.
    Obey her and leave your seat in the chariot.
CLYTAEMNESTRA I cannot waste time   1025
    Here outside: the sheep are already standing by the central hearth
    Ready to be killed at its fire,
    A pleasure I never expected to have.
    But you, if you are going to do anything I say, do not delay;
    If you do not understand or follow my meaning –   1030
    Rather than use words, *you* explain with some barbarian gesture.
CHORUS As a foreigner, she needs a good interpreter;
    Now she is behaving like an animal just captured.
CLYTAEMNESTRA She has gone mad and follows
    Her own crazed thoughts. She has left a newly captured city   1035
    And has just arrived here, but she will froth away her strength
    In blood before she learns how to bear the bridle.
    I will waste no more words only to be insulted.

FIRST *KOMMOS* (1042–1148)

A kommos *is a lament between a character and the Chorus. Here Cassandra laments both past deaths and imminent ones, including her own; the Chorus' responses are both prosaic and puzzled.*

Metre of the First *Kommos*

Conventionally both character and Chorus sing in lyric (see **Metre** page 14) during a *kommos*, but this is not the case here. In the first half (1042–89) Cassandra sings in lyric – often used in passages of emotional intensity and here reflecting Cassandra's anguish as she experiences her visions – while the Chorus speak in the iambic metre of ordinary dialogue. In the second half (1090–1148) the metres are reversed: Cassandra gradually becomes more calm, which is reflected in her use of a mixture of lyric and iambic. The Chorus, however, gradually become more worried and this is reflected in their use of a combination of iambic and lyric first, then solely lyric.

1042 Ah no, ah no The text here (and at 1046) reads *ototototoi popoi da*, a series of meaningless sounds. When Cassandra finally speaks (1051), it is clear that her previous silence (1017–41) was deliberate, for she speaks in Greek.

● Could the original exclamation be left to stand in a modern production? Does it have any power of its own?

Apollo

1045 He will not draw near The Chorus object that it is inappropriate for Apollo, the god of light and of purification, to have any dealings with the darkness of death or taint of mourning (1045, 1048–9). Cassandra addresses him with the epithet 'God at the doorway' (1051). Apollo was thought to guard the way to and from one's house; a piece of stone often stood at the entranceway as his symbol, and there are several vase-paintings showing this stone as part of the stage scenery.

Cassandra and Apollo

1052 Appalling as you ruin me once again Apollo, god of prophecy, conceived a desire for Cassandra and granted her the power of prophecy. When Cassandra then refused the god's advances, he decreed that although he could not withdraw his gift and she would retain her ability to foresee the future, no one would ever believe her predictions (1173–84). The Greek root *apoll-* means 'hurt' or 'destroy', lending itself to a pun (see note on 662) on the name Apollo.

CHORUS I feel sorry for her and will not be angry.

Come, you poor girl, leave your chariot; 1040

Yield to necessity and try on your new yoke.

CASSANDRA Ah no, ah no, for pity's sake no,

Apollo, Apollo.

CHORUS Why cry 'ah no' to Apollo?

He will not draw near a person in grief. 1045

CASSANDRA Ah no, ah no, for pity's sake no,

Apollo, Apollo.

CHORUS Once again with ominous words she calls on the god

Who must not be present in times of grief.

CASSANDRA Apollo, Apollo, 1050

God at the doorway, my Apollo,

Appalling as you ruin me once again.

*Cassandra, from the
National Theatre
production, London,
1981.*

1054 even in the mind of a slave   The Chorus are surprised that
Cassandra's divine gift of prophecy (see **Cassandra and Apollo** page
82) did not desert her at the same time as her royal status.

Cassandra's first vision (1055–70)

Cassandra has a vision of Atreus' feast (see Background to the story) *and*
Thyestes eating his own children (1061–3, 1066–8).

1058 house of the Atreidae   The Chorus take Cassandra's questions
(1057) literally. Their plain and prosaic comments (1058–9, 1069–70,
1083–4) in this part of the scene contrast with Cassandra's powerful
poetic utterances.

Cassandra's second vision (1071–1100)

Cassandra now has visions of a crime yet to be committed (1071–2), the
murder of a husband in his bath by his wife (1079–80, 1100).

1076 I do not follow   Cassandra urgently tries to warn the Chorus of
a great crime that is imminent, but the Chorus repeatedly fail to grasp
her meaning. The Chorus can understand Cassandra's first (1077) and
third visions (1133–4) but not her second.
- Is Cassandra's second vision so difficult to comprehend? Is there a
  reason why the Chorus might not want to follow this vision in
  particular?
- How does the Chorus' exasperating failure to understand
  Cassandra at this point affect the dramatic tension?

CHORUS It seems she will pronounce on her own misfortunes.
Divine inspiration remains even in the mind of a slave.
CASSANDRA   Apollo, Apollo,   1055
                  God at the doorway, my Apollo,
        Ah, where have you led me? What house is this?
CHORUS The house of the Atreidae; that I can tell you,
If you really do not know – and you will find it to be true.
CASSANDRA   Ah, ah,   1060
            Hating the gods and witness to many
                Foul and incestuous murders,
    Where men are butchered and floors spattered with blood.
CHORUS This stranger tracks like a hound,
Sniffing out murders she has yet to uncover.   1065
CASSANDRA Yes, here is the evidence to convince me:
            These children who weep for their murder,
        Their roasted flesh that was eaten by their father.
CHORUS Of course we have heard of your fame
As a seer: but we are not looking for prophecies.   1070
CASSANDRA Ah no, god no! What is she plotting?
            What is this new suffering? Great,
        Great is the crime that she plots in the house,
        Unbearable to the family, past healing, yet help
                    Stands far off.   1075
CHORUS These last prophecies I do not follow, though
I did understand those before: the whole city cries them out.
CASSANDRA Alas, wretched woman, will this be fulfilled?
            She is washing in his bath the husband
        Who shares her bed – how shall I say how it ends?   1080
    It will not be long now; hand over hand reaches out,
                Stretching forward.

1086 net See **The net** page 32.

1088 his murder; now let insatiable family feud This murder will form a link in the chain of revenge for murder within the family (see **A second cycle of vengeance** page 98). The feud is personified (see **Impersonal forces** page 34), crying out in exultation at the strife that is to ensue.

1089 stoning is considered an appropriate punishment for the murder of a king, because such a crime affects everyone and stoning is a form of punishment in which everyone can take part (1588). Cassandra's cries reach some sort of climax as she envisages Agamemnon's death and its repercussions.

1092 My blood turns yellow The Chorus are alarmed and break into lyric (see **Metre of the First *Kommos*** page 82). They believe that when a man dies, fear causes his blood to rush to the heart: we say nowadays that blood drains *from* the heart. As now, yellow is the colour associated with fear.

1098 black-horned cunning The images of animal and human merge. The word 'cunning' refers to the cunning of the wife in her scheming; 'black-horned' may suggest a 'dark' purpose.

1100 I tell you The first time Cassandra addresses the Chorus.

Cassandra's third vision (1107–43)
Cassandra's final vision is of her own death; the Chorus are shocked and alarmed.

1111 borne away by the god The Chorus believe that Cassandra's powers, a gift from Apollo (see **Cassandra and Apollo** page 82), have robbed her of her reason.

1115 'Itys, Itys' The Chorus refer to the story of Procne. Procne was married to King Tereus, but he conceived a desire for her sister Philomela. Having raped Philomela, he cut out her tongue so that she would be unable to tell Procne, but she nevertheless managed to get a message through by embroidering the act on a piece of cloth. To avenge her sister, Procne killed Itys, her own son by Tereus, and served him to her husband in a pie. Tereus discovered this and was on the point of killing both sisters, but was suddenly changed by the gods into a hoopoe, while Philomela and Procne were turned into a swallow and a nightingale respectively. The Chorus liken Cassandra to Procne in her nightingale form, since both sing a plaintive, discordant song; she resembles Philomela also – as a victim of male desire.

CHORUS I still do not understand; for now I am confused
By these riddles with their obscure predictions.

CASSANDRA Ah, ah, what now, what now, what is this that I see?   1085
A net from Hades.
No, the net is the woman that shares his bed, shares the guilt
Of his murder; now let insatiable family feud
Wail its triumph at this sacrifice that demands a stoning.

CHORUS What is this Fury you summon   1090
To raise its cry in the house? Your words chill me.
My blood turns yellow racing straight to my heart,
As when a man falls by the spear –
It reaches its end with the rays of a life as it sets;
Destruction moves quickly.   1095

CASSANDRA Ah, ah, look, look, keep the bull away
From its mate; catching him in a robe,
With black-horned cunning
She strikes; back he falls in the vessel full of water.
I tell you the bath is now a murderous trap.   1100

CHORUS I would not claim to be skilled in prophetic
Utterances, but this sounds like something terrible.
What good news for mankind
Ever comes from predictions? The arts of the prophets,
Full of words of disaster,   1105
Teach us to fear.

CASSANDRA Alas, alas, what horrors are destined this wretch?
It is for my suffering I pour out my lament.
Why did you bring me here, wretch that I am –
Simply to share in your death? What else?   1110

CHORUS You are out of your mind, borne away by the god.
You cry out for yourself
A tune without tune, like the shrill nightingale's
Insatiable cry: alas, with disconsolate heart
She moans 'Itys, Itys', his death full of pain   1115
For both parents.

1123 high-pitched notes The Chorus' words give some clue to the style of Cassandra's song.

1127 the marriage of Paris Cassandra is Paris' sister.

1131 Cocytus and Acheron are two rivers in the Underworld.

1139 my father's sacrifices It is unlikely that Priam would have been free to make sacrifices of sheep or cattle outside Troy's walls during the Trojan War; therefore this probably refers to the time before it.

1142 inexorable suffering indicates that the fall of Troy could not be averted (665); this is certainly accepted in the *Iliad* (*xii*, 15), where it is stated that Troy will fall in the tenth year of the war.

CASSANDRA Ah, ah, for the life of the shrill nightingale;
　　　　　　The gods wrapped her body in wings
　　And a sweet life spared further tears:
　　But for me there waits the cut from a double-edged blade.　　1120
CHORUS From where does this rush of prophecies come,
　　　　　　Such pain without purpose?
　　Why beat out these fears to a rhythm of high-pitched notes
　　　　　　And cries of ill-omen?
　　　　　　Where have you found the ominous signs　　1125
　　　　　　Marking the path of your prophecies?
CASSANDRA Oh the marriage, the marriage of Paris that killed
　　All his loved ones! Oh the waters of my native Scamander!
　　　　　　In time gone by I was raised and grew up
　　　　　　Round your banks, wretch that I am;　　1130
　　But now, it seems, round the banks of Cocytus and Acheron
　　I will soon be singing my prophecies.
CHORUS What are these words you have uttered all too clear?
　　　　　　A child could hear them and understand.
　　　　　　I am stung to the quick,　　1135
　　When you weep for your terrible fate so piteously:
　　　　　　It breaks me to hear it.
CASSANDRA Ah, the pain, the pain of a city so utterly destroyed!
　　Oh, my father's sacrifices in front of its towers,
　　　　　　So many animals from our pastures killed;　　1140
　　　　　　But they provided no cure
　　For the city's inexorable suffering;
　　And I too will soon spill my warm blood on the ground.
CHORUS 　This follows closely what you said before.
　　　　　　Some malevolent *daimōn*　　1145
　　Comes down on you hard and compels you to sing
　　Of a pitiful ordeal that will end in your death.
　　　　　　As to the end – I am lost.

Cassandra becomes calm (1149–1301)

Cassandra explains the visions she has just undergone in clearer and calmer language: the feast of Atreus (1188–93), Agamemnon's death (1200–2), her own death (1231–4), though she still experiences occasional agitations (1185–7, 1227–8). The scene ends when she goes inside the palace.

1151 like a wind appearing at sunrise Cassandra compares the current troubled situation to a turbulent sea: just as at sunrise the wind suddenly gets up and stirs the waves to swell towards the sun (1152), so now her visions reveal the imminent calamity looming ever larger (1153).

1154 No longer will I teach in riddles Cassandra claims to speak more clearly now, but she uses three metaphors in the first eight lines of her speech: the newly wed bride (1149–50); the sea (1151–2); and the hunt (1155–6).

Furies' vigil

1157 a choir Cassandra is able to see the pack of Furies (*Erinyes*, see **The Furies** page 8), who watch over the palace as a consequence of the blood-feud between Atreus and Thyestes; this ghoulish image of the Furies taking possession of the house conjures up a world of black supernatural horror. These are 'family Furies' (1160) who demand revenge for the death of a family member: in this case Atreus has murdered his own nephews and nieces, Thyestes' children. The Furies also remember Thyestes' adultery (see *Background to the story*) with his brother Atreus' wife, 'That first crime' (1163–4).

1167 Bear me witness and swear Another piece of legal imagery (see **Legal imagery** page 6). The victim of a crime could call out to a passer-by to witness that he had been wronged; the latter was then bound to appear in court if required.

1182 Loxias is an epithet of Apollo, derived from the Greek root *log-*, meaning 'speech' or 'word' and signifying his oracular role.

CASSANDRA   No longer, then, shall my prophecy peep out
From its veil like some newly wed bride.   1150
Bright like a wind appearing at sunrise,
And swelling like a wave into the sunlight,
Its end will be misery far greater than this.
No longer will I teach in riddles;
Be you my witness as I run down this trail   1155
And follow the scent of crimes committed long ago.
There is a choir that never leaves this house,
Of one voice but not harmonious: for they speak ill.
Indeed, they have drunk human blood
And grown more bold: the troupe of family Furies   1160
Haunts the halls, hard to evict.
Laying siege to the house, they sing their song of
That first crime and each in turn spits in loathing
On the man who defiled his brother's bed.
Have I missed the mark? Has this archer caught her prey?   1165
Or am I a bogus prophet, a pedlar of lies knocking at your door?
Bear me witness and swear that I do know the story,
The age-old wrongdoings of this house.
CHORUS   What comfort would an oath, truly pledged, be?
But you astonish me: 1170
Though raised across the sea, you are right
In what you say about a foreign city, as if you had been here.
CASSANDRA   The prophet Apollo placed this power in me.
CHORUS   Was the god really so smitten with desire?
CASSANDRA   Before now I was ashamed to talk about this.   1175
CHORUS   Everyone is more ... delicate in good times.
CASSANDRA   Then – he wrestled me hard as he breathed his desire.
CHORUS   And did you then make love?
CASSANDRA   I gave him my promise, but tricked him.
CHORUS   Were you already possessed by your god-given skill?   1180
CASSANDRA   Already I predicted their sufferings to my people.
CHORUS   Then how were you not harmed by Loxias' anger?
CASSANDRA   No one believed anything I said after my offence.
CHORUS   Yet to us your prophecies seem convincing.

1185 Alas, alas, ah, ah   Cassandra returns briefly to her earlier exclamations. She is overcome by a vision of Thyestes eating his own children at the feast, which she again (1066–8) seems to see taking place in front of her. The more clearly Cassandra describes her visions (1154), the more gruesome and macabre they become (1190–3).

1194–5 a faint-hearted lion,/I tell you, is plotting   As a consequence of the terrible feast, someone from inside the palace – the lion is the emblem of the royal house at Argos (see **The mauling of Troy** page 62) – is waiting for Agamemnon's return and the chance for vengeance. The lion is not named, but identified as an adulterer (1195), and is faint-hearted because he stayed in Argos during the Trojan War. Cassandra also calls Agamemnon a lion (1230) and Clytaemnestra a lioness (1229). The fifth-century audience might well have recognised this allusion to Aegisthus (see note on 1230).

1199 hateful bitch   In the *Odyssey* Agamemnon also calls Clytaemnestra 'bitch-faced' (see *Background to the story*).

1202 female murders male   It is not unusual in Greek tragedies to find a determined and occasionally criminal heroine (e.g. Euripides' *Medea*), but in no other extant tragedy does a woman murder any man herself deliberately and with her own hands, let alone her husband or king. Clytaemnestra must be a monster (1203–5).

1204 Amphisbaina or some Scylla   The Amphisbaina is a monster about which not much is known now. The Scylla is a fearsome six-headed monster that lives in a cave above the sea and opposite the whirlpool Charybdis. Passing ships must avoid being sucked down by the whirlpool and therefore sail close to Scylla's cave. She then darts out and snatches sailors from their ships and eats them. In *Odyssey xii* Odysseus must sail his ship between the two and inevitably loses some of his men to Scylla.

1206 an angry mother   Cassandra sees Clytaemnestra's motive (1389) clearly.

1207 she cried out for joy   Cassandra has heard Clytaemnestra's exultant prayer (946–7), but this may be a reference to Clytaemnestra's cries of joy (see note on 28, line 568) when she heard the news that Agamemnon was on his way home, for Cassandra has the power to 'see' what she is not actually present to witness.

CASSANDRA Alas, alas, ah, ah, the agony: 1185
The terrible pain of true prophecy whirls up inside me again;
It confounds me with premonitions, premonitions of evil.
Look at these children sitting by the house
Like images in dreams.
Children dying at the hands of their kin – can it be? – 1190
Filling their hands with meat, their own flesh,
And seeming to proffer their organs and intestines, pitiful load,
And their father took a taste.
It is vengeance for this that a faint-hearted lion,
I tell you, is plotting: rolling in her bed, keeping house 1195
Against the return of the man who is now my master –
For I have to endure slavery's yoke.
The commander of the fleet and destroyer of Ilium,
He knows nothing of that hateful bitch's tongue;
She spoke and strung out her plea with fair-seeming intent, 1200
And by an evil twist of fate she will accomplish her stealthy murder.
Such is her daring: female murders male.
What should I call this hateful beast?
The Amphisbaina or some Scylla
Living among the rocks, a blight on sailors, 1205
Or an angry mother from Hades, breathing implacable war
Against her family? How she cried out for joy,
The all-daring one, as if in some battle-rout,
Pretending to rejoice in his safe homecoming.
It is the same if I do not convince you at all – what of it? 1210
The future will come: and soon those of you present now
Will pity me and say I was too true a prophet.

CHORUS Thyestes feasting on his children's flesh:
That I understood and shuddered at; and I am gripped by terror
When I hear those events not imagined but true; 1215
But as I listen to the rest, I stumble and lose the scent.

CASSANDRA I am saying: you will see Agamemnon dead.

CHORUS Wretched girl, put your ominous talk to rest.

CASSANDRA The Healer does not influence what I say now.

CHORUS Not if it will happen; but I pray it will not. 1220

CASSANDRA You pray, but their concern is murder.

The murderer's identity

1223 You have misunderstood   If there was any lingering uncertainty as to the identity of Agamemnon's murderer, the clues have now come thick and fast (1202, 1206, 1209). The Chorus, however, still believe that his murderer will be a man (1222).

● Do Cassandra's words leave any room for doubt?

1226 Pythian oracles   See **Pythian Apollo** page 42.

1228 Lyceian Apollo!   The meaning of the epithet 'Lyceian' is uncertain: it may denote a connection with the land of Lycia or may derive from the Greek for a wolf (*lukos*) or for light (*lukē*). Apollo is often associated with shepherds and would use his bow to help them by killing wolves; in some legends he himself tends a flock of sheep. He is also god of the sun.

1230 a wolf   Though he was a lion before (1194) Aegisthus is now a wolf, in contrast with the true lions (1229–30) of the rightful royal household and perhaps emphasising his furtive nature, inferior to that of the brave lion.

Cassandra's sacred apparel

1236 this staff and the bands   The staff and bands (usually made of wool) worn around the neck are signs of Cassandra's sacred status. After receiving the gift of prophecy, Cassandra wears the sacred robes, but no one will believe her predictions; thus she wanders around Troy in a state of mental and physical despair, laughed at (1242–3) by those who should have been her friends (see **Friends and enemies** page 102). Cassandra now tears off the symbols of her craft to spite Apollo.

● Why does Cassandra remark that Apollo himself is stripping her?

1246 the seer has claimed his seeress   As god of prophecy and as frustrated lover, Apollo claims the life of Cassandra.

1248 my father's altar   Cassandra's comment is poignant because Priam was killed at his altar when Troy was sacked (see **The mauling of Troy** page 62). There was no executioner's block in Greece: the 'butcher's block' is solely for chopping up meat.

1249 sacrifice   The word has by now an ominous and ironic significance. Agamemnon sacrificed Iphigeneia (210–23); Clytaemnestra has invited Cassandra in to be present at a sacrifice (1006–7, 1026); Cassandra has already described the killing of Agamemnon as a sacrifice (1089); now she describes her own and Agamemnon's murder brutally, in terms of a macabre and unholy ritual (see **Sacrifice** page 22).

CHORUS What man is preparing this horror?

CASSANDRA You have misunderstood my prophecies completely.

CHORUS Because I cannot see any way for him to manage it.

CASSANDRA Yet I understand Greek all too well.   1225

CHORUS And the Pythian oracles, but still I find them difficult.

CASSANDRA Aagh! What fire! How it attacks me!

Oh no, no! Lyceian Apollo! I…! I…!

This two-footed lioness lies down

With a wolf, while her noble lion is away: 1230

She will kill me, wretch that I am. While mixing her medicine,

She throws in my payment along with her anger;

As she whets a sword for him, she boasts that

She will exact a murderous requital for my being brought here.

Why do I keep these things to mock me –   1235

And this staff and the bands of prophecy around my neck?

Before I myself die I will destroy you.

Good riddance to you. Lie there while I repay you.

Enrich with ruin some woman other than me.

See, Apollo himself strips me of   1240

My prophet's clothing. He watched me

Cause much laughter in these fineries

To empty friends not much different from enemies.

I wandered round like some scrounging vagrant

And endured taunts of beggar, half-starved wretch;   1245

And now the seer has claimed his seeress

And marched me off to this encounter with death:

Instead of my father's altar a butcher's block waits, bloodied

As I am hacked down in reeking prelude to the main sacrifice.

Agamemnon's avenger

1251–5 Cassandra explains that the gods have promised (1255) that Orestes (see **Orestes** page 66) will return to bring retribution for his father (1252): the obligation to avenge the dead Agamemnon will draw him back to Argos (1256).

1255 a coping-stone is placed on top of a finished wall to divert rain-water which would otherwise seep in: Cassandra implies that Orestes will put a cap on the murders in the house of Atreus. The image of water flowing away may evoke the blood that he will shed or the consequent blood-guilt that cannot be washed off.

1260 Escape sentence The Greeks have not paid for their sack of Troy (see **Legal imagery** page 6).

1269 ox driven on by a god Cassandra goes to her death like a sacrificial animal to the altar (see **Sacrifice** page 22, note on 1249). If the victim goes forwards without a struggle, it is taken as a sign that the god approves the sacrifice.

1275 a famous death The Chorus console Cassandra with the thought that though she must die, her death will be remembered (see **Glory** page 40). The Chorus express the same sentiment to Antigone in Sophocles' *Antigone* when she is condemned to death.

1283 Syrian incense accompanies the sacrifice (see note on 95). There is evidence of extensive trade in ancient times between various Greek cities and those in the East.

But at least we will not die without due honour from the gods: 1250
For another will come back to be our avenger,
A mother-killing son, bringing retribution for his father:
A wandering exile, displaced from this land,
Will return for his family to seal these killings
With a coping-stone. A great oath has been sworn by the gods   1255
That his father's body lying here will bring him back.
What can be the point of my grieving so pitifully?
I watched what happened to the city of Troy
As it happened, and saw those who took the city
Escape sentence by the judgement of the gods.   1260
I shall make a start by going in, I shall brave death.
These gates I address as if the gates of Hades:
I pray that I meet one fatal blow,
So that, as my blood flows out without a struggle,
I may close these eyes in an easy death.   1265

CHORUS   Most unhappy woman, but most wise too,
You have spoken at length. But if you genuinely
Know your own fate, how can you go bravely to the altar
Like some ox driven on by a god?

CASSANDRA   There is no escape, friends, and no time left.   1270
CHORUS   But one's final moments are the most prized.
CASSANDRA   That hour is come: I will gain little by flight.
CHORUS   Know you are strong because your heart is brave.
CASSANDRA   No fortunate person hears such words.
CHORUS   But a famous death is a blessing for mortals.   1275
CASSANDRA   O, father! You and your royal children!
CHORUS   What is the matter? What fear whirls you round?
CASSANDRA   Alas, alas.
CHORUS   Why do you cry alas, if not at some horror in your mind?
CASSANDRA   The house reeks of blood-dripping murder.   1280
CHORUS   No, no. That is the smell of the sacrifices at the hearth.
CASSANDRA   It smells just like the vapour from the grave.
CHORUS   So, not the Syrian incense enriching the house.

1287 some bird snared in the thicket To catch birds, nets are painted with lime and hidden in thickets: the hunted bird becomes entangled in the net and stuck on the glue-like lime.

1288 be my witness to this Cassandra can make this demand because she is a 'foreigner' (1291): foreigners have guest status (see **Hospitality** page 8) and therefore those rights and privileges.

1298–1301 mortal affairs... Even in prosperous times a man's 'good fortune' has as little substance as a 'shadow' and may quickly disappear, but in bad times, the whole 'picture' of his life may be quickly erased by a single disaster.

Fourth Episode (1005–1301)

Cassandra leaves the stage (1301), possibly accompanied by attendants (see **Clytaemnestra scene with Cassandra** page 80). Though a slave, she goes of her own free will (1261) and bravely (1268).

- This is the longest episode in the play so far. How does Aeschylus vary its pace to maintain tension?
- What role do the Chorus play?
- How clear is what Cassandra says? What is the effect of her frequent use of metaphor?
- Do your feelings about her change during the scene?
- How might Cassandra's entrance to the palace differ from Agamemnon's?

FOURTH CHORAL ODE (4TH *STASIMON*) (1302–13)

*The Chorus break into lyric (see **Metre** page 14, **Metre of the First Kommos** page 82) and seem set for a full-blown* stasimon. *In this way the timing of Agamemnon's death still comes as a surprise, even though the audience are expecting it, for his cry cuts off the* stasimon *abruptly.*

1304 home that men point at Men point at the splendid appearance of a home, which is made possible by the success (1302) of its owner.

A second cycle of vengeance

1309–11 The cycle of revenge (see **A cycle of vengeance** page 18) is inevitable. The 'bloodshed of times gone by' and 'those who have died' comprise the sacrifice of Iphigeneia, the killing of Thyestes' children and those who died at Troy. These deaths lead to the present murder of Agamemnon, which will in turn 'Cause others to die in revenge' for his murder (see **Agamemnon's avenger** page 96).

1313 that protects him A *daimōn* can protect as well as destroy (see *Daimōn* page 58).

CASSANDRA   Now I shall go and inside the house I shall weep
    For my fate and for Agamemnon's: enough of life.   1285
    Oh no, strangers.
    I do not, like some bird snared in the thicket, shiver from fear,
    But, as I am about to die, be my witness to this,
    A woman shall die for a woman – for me –
    And a mismarried man for a man shall fall.   1290
    I claim this as a foreigner and as one about to die.
CHORUS   You poor wretch, I pity you your god-ordained death.
CASSANDRA   I wish to make one more speech – or rather
    A requiem for myself; I pray to the sun,
    To this final light, that those who bring vengeance   1295
    Requite our enemies for my murder too –
    The killing of a slave, an easy conquest.
    Ah, mortal affairs: in times of good fortune
    You may compare them to a shadow; but in ill-fortune,
    A watery sponge wipes out the picture at a stroke.   1300
    For this more than anything else am I filled with a sense of pity.

CHORUS   Success is by nature something no man
      Has enough of; no one rejects it and keeps it
        Out from a home that men point at,
          Saying 'Enter here no more.'   1305
       The blessed gods even granted this man
        To capture the city of Priam.
    Honoured by the gods he arrives at his home,
   But if he now is to pay for the bloodshed of times gone by
       And by dying for those who have died   1310
        Cause others to die in revenge,
    Who then of mortals would boast he was born
With a *daimōn* that protects him, when he heard about this?

FIFTH EPISODE (1314–1548)

The Chorus discuss what they might do (1317–42) in response to Agamemnon's cries. Suddenly Clytaemnestra appears, with the bodies of the murdered Agamemnon and Cassandra. She boasts (1343–69) how she ensnared Agamemnon and killed him. The Chorus are horrified, but Clytaemnestra explains that Agamemnon had to pay for his sacrifice of Iphigeneia (1384–97) and for his insulting her by bringing Cassandra back (1411–20). The Chorus and Clytaemnestra then argue about the justice of Agamemnon's death (1421–1548) but reach no agreement.

Violence offstage

1314 in here – I have been stabbed   In tragedy violence on stage is rare. Either there are cries of violence offstage, to which the characters on stage react, or violent action is reported by a messenger shortly after it has taken place.

The Chorus debate

1341 we all agree to this   The Chorus in tragedy may discuss what they might do, but rarely do they in fact take any action.

- Is there any indication that Clytaemnestra's arrival interrupts some action on the Chorus' part?
- To what extent do the Chorus agree on what action they should take?
- How might the discussion (1317–42) be staged to illustrate their response to the situation?

Bodies on stage

Clytaemnestra now returns with the bodies of Agamemnon and Cassandra, possibly on the *ekkyklēma*, a low wooden platform on wheels, on which is laid out a tableau of the violent act that has occurred offstage. Were this not used, an alternative would be for the bodies to be positioned by the doorway according to custom, for much of this scene (1421–1548) relies on traditional mourning ritual. Often in tragedy a messenger reports violent events offstage (see above), but the audience here receive another surprise (see **Fourth Stasimon** page 98): Clytaemnestra boldly reports her killing of Agamemnon herself.

AGAMEMNON Aagh – in here – I have been stabbed – a fatal blow!

CHORUS Quiet! Who screams that he is wounded by a fatal blow? 1315

AGAMEMNON Aaagh, another – I have been stabbed again!

CHORUS From the screams of the king, I think the deed is done.

Still, together let us think of a safe course of action.

– I will tell you my suggestion:

Summon the citizens to bring help here to the house. 1320

– I think we should rush in as quickly as possible

And seize the freshly dripping sword to prove the deed.

– I too share your thoughts:

I vote we do something: the main thing is that there be no delay.

– It is clear to see: this is the prelude, 1325

A sign that they plan tyranny for the city.

– While we waste time, their hands do not sleep;

They trample the very name of hesitation to the ground.

– I know of no plan that I might sensibly suggest.

Even the man prepared to act must first think what to do. 1330

– That is my opinion too, since I know no way

To raise the dead man up again with words.

– Shall we drag out our lives by letting those

Who defile the house rule over us?

– That I could not bear – death is better: 1335

It is a milder fate than tyranny.

– Are we to divine that our master has been killed

With these screams as our proof?

– We must have certain knowledge when we speak about this,

For having certain knowledge is different from guessing. 1340

– I feel, then, that we all agree to this,

To find out for sure what has happened to Atreus' son.

1343–4 I have said many things to suit/The moment It now becomes clear that Clytaemnestra has either blatantly lied (594, 830–1, 859) or at the very least spoken with irony (see **Irony** page 48) for much of the play (481, 581–2, 884).

Friends and enemies
1345–6 injuries on those enemies/That pretended to be friends
The distinction between friends and enemies (1243) is important. It is a matter of pride and duty (and pleasure) to harm one's enemies, while one should help one's friends (*philoi* 'dear ones' – a term which includes anyone close, family or friend). The wish to be loyal to one's friends and to harm one's enemies is often voiced in tragedy. By allowing the sacrifice of Iphigeneia, Agamemnon broke the bonds of friendship (*philia*) and incurred Clytaemnestra's enmity.

The net
1353 I wrap him in a net without end Clytaemnestra starts to give her account of Agamemnon's murder, which Cassandra prophesied (1085–9, 1096–9). The 'net' may be a real net in which she traps him or perhaps a large cloth which is used like a fishing-net to entangle him (see **The net** page 32), or it may describe Clytaemnestra's own robe, mentioned by Cassandra (1097) and Aegisthus (1552). There is no mention of a net in the account of Agamemnon's death in the *Odyssey* (see *Background to the story*).

A thank-offering to Zeus
1357–8 a thank-you prayer/To Zeus Clytaemnestra daringly thanks Zeus – to whom she prayed (946) as Agamemnon went to his death – for the death of Agamemnon, conflating the traditional thank-offering to Zeus with the mourning libation (see note on 232) to Hades. The third offering at a sacrifice or less formal occasion is made to Zeus *Sōtēr* – 'guardian' or saviour. Clytaemnestra openly accords Hades – whom she calls 'Zeus of the Underworld' – both Zeus' title of *Sōtēr* and the third libation reserved for him. While it is normal to say a prayer while pouring a libation for the dead man, Clytaemnestra expresses pleasure at his death (1365) and she considers it fitting to do so, because Agamemnon, having agreed to the sacrifice of Iphigeneia, has now himself suffered a similar fate.

1362 the crops in the ecstasy Clytaemnestra imagines the joy crops feel as they produce their fruit and compares it to the ecstasy she experiences as she kills Agamemnon.

- How appropriate is Clytaemnestra's comparison? Does she imply that Zeus approves her actions? How do you react to the image?

CLYTAEMNESTRA In the past I have said many things to suit
The moment; now I shall not be ashamed to say the opposite;
How else is one to inflict injuries on those enemies   1345
That pretended to be friends, or rig up a net of troubles
Too high to jump over?
Long did I consider it, before the climax
Of this long feud arrived: for, though late, arrive it did.
I stand where I struck, by my work which is done.   1350
I ensured – and I will not deny it –
That he could not escape death, nor fend it off.
I wrap him in a net without end,
Like for fish, a robe deadly in its wealth.
Twice I strike and in the space of two screams   1355
His body collapsed on the spot, and as he lay fallen
I add a third, a thank-you prayer
To Zeus of the Underworld, guardian of the dead.
So he falls, driving the spirit out of him,
And as he gasps out his gushing death-blood,   1360
He sprays me with a dark shower of gory dew,
And I revel no less than the crops in the ecstasy
Zeus grants them when they give birth from their husks.
In this situation, you elders of Argos,
Rejoice, if you would rejoice; I glory in it.   1365
Could I but pour the libation he deserves over his corpse,
Then such would it be – and justly, all too justly.
This man filled the wine-bowl in his house with so much
Cursed misery – and he himself returned and drained it.

Clytaemnestra's brazenness

1370–1 How brazen/Your tongue!   Perhaps for the first time in the play Clytaemnestra speaks frankly, without irony or dissimulation (see **Irony** page 48, note on 1343–4). The Chorus are amazed.

- What is Clytaemnestra's predominant emotion as she gives the speech at lines 1343–69?
- Which parts seem brazen or outspoken?
- How might her actions or behaviour reflect her new openness?
- How much use of gesture would you have Clytaemnestra make as she describes Agamemnon's murder?

1372–3 woman/With no wits   Clytaemnestra is now able to respond to the Chorus' attacks on her sex (see **Male and female** page 30, **Glory** page 40) with more potency: she proudly asserts her responsibility for the killing (1376) and is triumphant at the justice of it (886, 1377).

1378 edible evil   The Chorus suppose that Clytaemnestra has taken some sort of drug to enable her to commit such a dreadful crime. The Chorus switch to lyric metre (see **Metre** page 14) to reflect the intensity of their emotions (see **Metre of the First *Kommos*** page 82).

1381–2 curses/Pronounced by the people   The citizens will curse Clytaemnestra and give effect to their judgement by banishing her (1382). The Chorus have already confirmed the effectiveness of people's curses (439–40).

Clytaemnestra's first defence (1384–97)

Clytaemnestra defends her actions, responding to the Chorus' likening the murder to a sacrifice (see note on 1249, line 1381). Agamemnon killed their child Iphigeneia: by calling her the 'most precious pain/Of my labour' (1389–90), Clytaemnestra emphasises the outrage to herself as a mother, in addition to his crime against their marriage. She challenges the Chorus to say why they did not protest at that murder (1391–2).

1390 Thracian winds   The winds from Strymon (178) which held up the fleet and later destroyed much of it on the return voyage (635, see map on page x).

Pollution of bloodshed

1392 pollution   By killing Iphigeneia Agamemnon incurred religious and social pollution, a fitting punishment for which is banishment: this would protect Argos from guilt by association. In Sophocles' *Oedipus Tyrannus*, Thebes suffers a plague because the city harbours Oedipus when he has killed his own father.

CHORUS We are astonished at your speech! How brazen   1370
   Your tongue! What words you crow over your husband!

CLYTAEMNESTRA You challenge me as if I were a woman
   With no wits, but I speak with a fearless heart to those
   Who know – and whether you wish to praise or blame me,
   Makes no difference – this is Agamemnon, my husband,   1375
   Now a corpse, the work of this my right hand,
   The craftsman of justice. That is how things stand.

CHORUS   What edible evil that grows in the ground
        Or that springs from the rippling sea to be drunk,
                Did you taste, woman, that   1380
   You performed this sacrifice, cut loose and threw away curses
   Pronounced by the people? You will be banished from the city,
        A mighty abhorrence to her citizens.

CLYTAEMNESTRA Now you condemn me to banishment
   From the city with curses pronounced by her people, abhorrent   1385
   To her citizens. *Then* you put up no opposition to this man:
   He cared as little as for the death of an animal
   From his ample flocks in the fleecy pastures,
   When he sacrificed his own child, most precious pain
   Of my labour, as a charm for Thracian winds.   1390
   Was it not he you should have driven from this land
   As payment for his pollution? Yet when you hear what
   I have done, you are a stern judge. But I say to you:
   When you make threats like these, know that
   I am equally prepared: let that man rule who defeats me   1395
   By force; but if god decrees the contrary,
   Late though your schooling may be, you will learn to see sense.

1398 Your schemes are ambitious   The Chorus have no answer to
Clytaemnestra's challenge (1391–2) but respond to her threats
(1394–7) by remarking that Clytaemnestra cannot escape the
inevitable cycle of each murder requiring another in revenge (see **A
second cycle of vengeance** page 98). She must atone for the blow that
killed Agamemnon by receiving a blow that will kill her (1403); her
'loved ones' or friends (see **Friends and enemies** page 102) will not be
able to help her.

Clytaemnestra's second defence (1404–20)

*Continuing her explanation that she killed Agamemnon for his sacrifice
of Iphigeneia (1389), Clytaemnestra confidently claims to have the
support of the forces of Justice (1377, 1405) and Destruction (see
Impersonal forces page 34) and the Furies (1406). She will fear nothing
while Aegisthus is by her side; thus she introduces Aegisthus by name for
the first time (1408). Aegisthus is Thyestes' surviving son and
Clytaemnestra's lover; in her eyes he is now the master of the house and
hearth (see **The hearth** page 54). It therefore seems hypocritical that in
almost the same breath, she then adds new justification for the murder:
Agamemnon was disloyal to her not only as a mother but also as a wife.
He had a mistress at Troy (1412) and has brought home a mistress too
(1414) – note her sexual bitterness (1414–16).*

- How might these two speeches (1384–97, 1404–20) in her defence
  affect the audience's sympathies? Are the arguments of each equally
  valid and effective?

1408 Aegisthus lights the fire in my hearth   Clytaemnestra claims
that she fears nothing while Aegisthus is at her side (1407) and
lighting the fire in her hearth, though lighting and keeping alight the
fire in the hearth was for a woman to do (**Male and female** page 118);
perhaps the sexual innuendo counts for more than the literal meaning
in this instance.

1412 Chryses' girls   In the *Iliad* Agamemnon is given Chryseis,
daughter of Chryses, as a prize when the Achaeans sack the town of
Chryse near Troy, and claims to prefer her to his wife (*Iliad i*, 106–15).
Though Agamemnon was given one of Chryses' daughters only,
Clytaemnestra exaggerates out of bitterness.

1419 dirge for her death   In the *Odyssey xi* Agamemnon explains to
Odysseus in the Underworld that his most pitiful moment as he died
was hearing Cassandra's cry as she too was killed (see *Background to
the story*).

CHORUS   Your schemes are ambitious,
                Your words full of arrogance. Just as
Your mind is unhinged from your blood-streaked exploits,   1400
            So streaks of blood stand out in your eyes.
    Retribution still awaits you: deprived of your loved ones,
            You must pay for a blow with a blow.

CLYTAEMNESTRA   Hear the oaths it is my right to swear:
    By the Justice struck for my daughter,   1405
    By Destruction and by the Erinys for whom I murdered this man,
    My hopes do not walk the halls of fear,
    While Aegisthus lights the fire in my hearth;
    He has my interests at heart, now as before.
    No small shield of courage is that man for me.   1410
    Here lies the man who ruined me, his wife,
    Who melted the hearts of Chryses' girls at Ilium,
    And here is the prisoner and prophet,
    This man's bedfellow, soothsayer,
    Loyal concubine; they wore away   1415
    The ships' benches together and their acts do not go unrewarded:
    For thus he lies, as his lover does too,
    Who so recently sang like a swan
    A dirge for her death; he brought her along
    To add relish to his enjoyment of my bed.   1420

SECOND *KOMMOS* (1421–1548)

The Second Kommos *comprises an emotional exchange between the Chorus and Clytaemnestra. However, like the first, in which Cassandra uttered a lament for those not yet dead, this* kommos *also differs from convention (see* **Ritual mourning** *page 114). The Second* Kommos *is a reverse of the first (see* **Metre of the First** Kommos *page 82): in the first Cassandra sang in lyric and then switched to iambic; here Clytaemnestra speaks in iambic and then switches to lyric.*

1426 because of a woman   Helen (see note on 431).

1431 one last flower of remembrance   may stand for Agamemnon's death, which rounds off the tally of deaths Helen has caused. The 'blood that would not be washed out' may refer to any or all of: the blood shed at Atreus' feast, the blood of Iphigeneia and the blood of those killed at Troy.

1434 A powerful spirit of Strife   See **Impersonal forces** page 34.

1438 a single woman   Clytaemnestra cannot agree that all the responsibility for those who died at Troy lies with Helen, though in the *Odyssey* Odysseus complains to Agamemnon that so many Achaeans were killed because of Helen.

● Who else might Clytaemnestra think shares the responsibility?

The *daimōn* of the house

1441–61   The Chorus claim that the *daimōn* (see **Daimōn** page 58) of the house of Atreus has now attacked both branches of the house (1442), namely those of Menelaus and Agamemnon. The *daimōn* wields its 'power through women' (1443), as Clytaemnestra and Helen both bring ruin to their respective husbands, Agamemnon and Menelaus; in the *Odyssey* Odysseus uses a similar phrase (see *Background to the story*). Clytaemnestra agrees with the Chorus and claims that this same *daimōn* has been 'fattened three times' (1450), perhaps because it has thrice fed on family blood (Thyestes' children, Iphigeneia, Agamemnon).

1442 Tantalus' line   Tantalus was an ancestor of Agamemnon (see *Genealogical table*, page ix).

CHORUS   Alas, what death can come quickly,
          Without too much pain and without a long vigil,
             And bring us unending sleep for ever,
                Now the kindest of guardians
                   Is brought down,   1425
          After suffering so much because of a woman?
             At the hands of a woman he has died.

                        Alas for
          The insanity of Helen: though one woman,
             You destroyed so many, so very many souls   1430
Beneath Troy. Now you have laid one last flower of remembrance
             For the blood that would not be washed out.
                Once before now there was in the house
          A powerful spirit of Strife that brought a man misery.

CLYTAEMNESTRA Do not pray for the release of death,   1435
          As though you were burdened by these events;
             Do not turn your anger on Helen
          As destroyer of men, as though a single woman
             Destroyed the souls of many Danaan men,
                And caused pain that will not heal.   1440

CHORUS   You, *daimōn* who swoop down on this house
             And both branches of Tantalus' line,
                You wield your power through women
          Whose minds are alike and it gnaws at my heart;
                   Standing over the body   1445
                Like some odious crow out of tune,
                She glories in singing her song.

CLYTAEMNESTRA Now with that opinion you hit the mark,
                Invoking the family *daimōn*,
                   Fattened three times;   1450
          From him comes the blood-licking lust
             That is nursed in the belly; before an old
                Pain has abated, new pus appears.

1458 it must be from Zeus Zeus (see **Zeus** page 6) is the original cause of all things (1459–61) and therefore he must ultimately be responsible for Agamemnon's murder, though it was the work of human hand (1468).

Clytaemnestra as avenging spirit

1475 Took on the appearance Clytaemnestra has hitherto claimed full responsibility for the murder (1376). Now she claims that she embodies a spirit of vengeance, which has assumed her shape. The Chorus will not let her disclaim responsibility in this way (1478–9); she bears her own guilt, even if the blood-guilt bequeathed by Atreus (1480–1) required Agamemnon's murder in vengeance for the murder of Thyestes' children (1476–7).

- Do you think Clytaemnestra is wavering in the face of the Chorus' accusations?
- Does her claim to be possessed by a Fury lessen her responsibility (see **Paris' responsibility** page 34) for her actions?

1482 Black Ares Perhaps black with blood (which is often described as black in Greek literature) or black because his mood is grim.

Clytaemnestra stands triumphant over the bodies of Agamemnon and Cassandra. Scene from the National Theatre production, London, 1981.

CHORUS   You speak of a powerful *daimōn*
That is heavy in its anger at this house.   1455
Alas, alas, what a terrible tale of
Ruinous misfortune unsated –
Ah, alas, it must be from Zeus,
All-causing, all-achieving;
What is ever accomplished among men without Zeus?   1460
What is there that is not god-ordained?

Ah, ah, my king, my king,
How shall I weep for you?
What can I say in my devotion?
In an ungodly death you breathed out your life   1465
And so in this spider's web you lie trapped,
Alas, alas,
Brought down by a double-edged knife in her hand
In a death of deception.

CLYTAEMNESTRA You insist that this deed is my own,   1470
And believe me to be
The wife of Agamemnon;
But an ancient avenger, bitter at Atreus
Who gave that vile feast,
Took on the appearance of the wife of this corpse,   1475
And sacrificed a full-grown man to those children,
Offering him up as payment.

CHORUS   Who will bear witness that you are
Innocent of this murder? How could they? How?
Even though an avenger, the bequest of his father,   1480
May have been your accomplice.
Black Ares rampages
In a river of family blood:
As he moves forward, he will bring justice
For the blood congealed in the meat of those children.   1485

1497–1504 Clytaemnestra returns to the sacrifice of Iphigeneia (1387–92). Agamemnon had to die for killing his daughter, who was just as much her child as his (1389–90, 1500).

1509 no longer falls lightly The light falling of blood may be a metaphorical reference to the visions of murder that Cassandra had; the light fall has now become a rainstorm, namely the actual murders of Agamemnon and Cassandra. The Chorus now fear a blood-bath, for in the cycle of vengeance (see **A second cycle of vengeance** page 98) the murders of Agamemnon and Cassandra demand the death of their murderer – this is justice (1510) – and Clytaemnestra's death (1252) thus becomes inevitable. This is the Fate (1511) Cassandra has already prophesied (1250–6).

Clytaemnestra defends her murder of Agamemnon and Cassandra. Scene from the National Theatre production, London, 1991.

Ah, ah, my king, my king,
How shall I weep for you?
What can I say in my devotion?
In an ungodly death you breathed out your life
And so in this spider's web you lie trapped,   1490
Alas, alas,
Brought down by a double-edged knife in her hand
In a death of deception.

CLYTAEMNESTRA I would not say he was trapped
At his death or brought down   1495
By my double-edged knife in a death of deception.
Did *he* not visit
A death by deception on our house?
To Iphigeneia much wept for,
My child by him and raised by me,   1500
He did something she did not deserve.
Suffering as he now deserves, let him make no proud boasts
Down in Hades. Slain by the sword,
He paid with his death for what he began.

CHORUS   I am bewildered which way to turn,   1505
Deprived of thought's resourceful care,
While the house is collapsing.
I am afraid of the house-shaking beat
Of the rainstorm of blood; it no longer falls lightly.
Justice is sharpened for yet further harm   1510
On other whetstones of Fate.

Ritual mourning

1515 Who will mourn him? The women of the family normally wash and dress the body of a dead man, ready for him to be burned or buried. It is also their role to sing the formal laments and make the appropriate libations: to leave a corpse unmourned or unburied is to treat it, and so the gods of the Underworld, with dishonour. Although it is the women's duty, it is the Chorus who lament the dead Agamemnon (1462–9, repeated 1486–93). Each stanza of their heart-felt lamentation, however, is countered by a stanza of accusation or exultation from Clytaemnestra, who in bitter dramatic irony shares the form of their lament but not its content. She does promise Agamemnon a burial, but one without proper mourning (1525–6). In the *Odyssey xi* Agamemnon relates how Clytaemnestra could not bear even to close his eyes or mouth – basic acts of respect at a man's death – when he died (see *Background to the story*).

1529–30 At the ford of/The fast-flowing river Souls of the dead are ferried across the river Styx to the Underworld by Charon the ferryman: it is at this crossing-point that Iphigeneia will rush to embrace her father.
● What is Clytaemnestra's tone as she describes this imaginary scene?

1536 The doer must suffer The Chorus hold firm to the principle (1403) that each action has its inevitable consequence and that this law (1535) is upheld by Zeus (see **Zeus** page 6).

A pact with the *daimōn*

1540 sworn this agreement Clytaemnestra knows that 'the doer must suffer' (1536), but has sought an agreement with the *daimōn* (see **Daimōn** page 58) attacking the house (1541): she will accept all that has happened and give up her share of the royal wealth, if only that *daimōn* will now go elsewhere and persecute some other house (1542–8).
● Clytaemnestra is sure that justice is on her side (1367, 1377). Why does she need to make a pact with the *daimōn* about her future?
● Cassandra has foretold that Agamemnon's murder will be avenged (1251–2) and the Chorus have explained that Zeus' law is that 'The doer must suffer' (1536). How do Clytaemnestra's future prospects affect your attitude towards her?

1541 Pleisthenes is an ancestor of Agamemnon (see *Genealogical table*, page ix).

Clytaemnestra defends her actions (1343–1548)

● What are the main points of Clytaemnestra's defence? How convincing are they? How effectively do the Chorus put them to the test?
● What sort of person does Clytaemnestra seem now? Were there any indications of this earlier in the play?

Oh earth, earth, how I wish you had received me,
Before I could see him bedded down
In his silver-walled bath.
Who will bury him? Who will mourn him?   1515
Or will you dare to do this, after killing your own husband,
Loudly to mourn him,
To do his soul honours without honour,
An unjust return for his great deeds?
Who will pour out praise for a man like a god   1520
Together with tears at his tomb
And grieve with genuine feeling?

CLYTAEMNESTRA It is not for you to concern yourselves
With this; at my hand
He fell and died and we will inter him,   1525
Though not to the wailing of those from his house.
But his daughter Iphigeneia will go gladly
To meet him, her father, as she should,
At the ford of
The fast-flowing river of pain;   1530
She will embrace him and show him her love.

CHORUS   Reproach confronts reproach,
The struggle to judge is a hard one.
Plunderer is plundered, the killer pays in full.
While Zeus remains on his throne, this remains true: 1535
The doer must suffer. It is the law.
Who is there to cast the seed of the curse from the house?
The family is glued to destruction.

CLYTAEMNESTRA With truth do you make that prediction;
So now I have sworn this agreement   1540
With the *daimōn* of the house of Pleisthenes:
I am willing to accept what has happened,
Hard though it is to bear, but as for the future,
He should go away from this house and wear away
Some other line with the murder of its kin.   1545
It is quite enough for me to have a small part
Of its wealth, if I can drive from our house
The madness of murdering our own.

EXODOS (1549–1645)

The Exodos *is both the final scene in a tragedy and the actual exit of the Chorus, who always leave the stage last. Aegisthus enters. He expresses his satisfaction (1549–83) at Agamemnon's murder, thinking it just retribution for the killing of Thyestes' children by Agamemnon's father Atreus, and he claims that he planned the murder. The Chorus express their disdain and Aegisthus responds with threats (1584–1625). They almost come to blows, but Clytaemnestra intervenes. She and Aegisthus then leave.*

Aegisthus

1549 O kindly light of a day that brings justice   Aegisthus' arrival is sudden and unannounced (see **Character introduction** page 42). He has been mentioned by name only once (1408) – as new master of the palace. He is accompanied by soldiers (1623); while he speaks, Clytaemnestra remains silent, until she feels she must intervene (1626). Aegisthus, like Agamemnon (785–7) and Clytaemnestra (1367, 1377), is sure that justice is on his side.

● How does the arrival of soldiers affect the mood of the scene?

Inherited guilt

1554 He pays in full for the schemes of his father's hand   The Chorus have warned that payment for guilt may be passed down the generations (359); Aegisthus expresses the same belief: Atreus did not pay for his crime (killing Thyestes' children), so it is right that his son Agamemnon should, and right that Aegisthus (as Thyestes' son) be the one to exact payment (1576).

Suppliants

1559–60 suppliant/Of the hearth   When a person sits by the hearth (see **The hearth** page 54) in the position of a suppliant, the head of the household (see **The house** page 2) is bound by the rights due a guest (see **Hospitality** page 8) and suppliant to protect him from any threat. Zeus oversees these rights and is expected to punish any breach. By returning as a suppliant, Thyestes saved himself (1561) but reckoned without Atreus killing his children.

1564 A day for the carving of meat   Meat is expensive, so eating it is often associated with a special occasion or celebration.

1572 Pelops   is the grandfather of both Agamemnon and Aegisthus (see *Genealogical table*, page ix). For Pleisthenes (1574) see note on 1541.

1576 I be the one to tailor   Clytaemnestra speaks of herself as a craftsman of justice (1377); now Aegisthus describes himself as a tailor of murder. They both see artistry in the planning and execution of Agamemnon's murder.

AEGISTHUS O kindly light of a day that brings justice;

 Now I would say that the gods, as avengers of mortals,   1550

 Do indeed look down from above at the pain on earth,

 For I see this man lying here in a robe

 Woven by Furies and it pleases me;

 He pays in full for the schemes of his father's hand.

 When Atreus, this man's father, ruled this land,   1555

 He drove Thyestes, my father – let that be clear –

 His own brother, out from both city and home,

 Since he was a rival to his authority.

 The wretched Thyestes came back, but as a suppliant

 Of the hearth, so as not to meet his death   1560

 And thereby bloody the soil of his fathers: thus he saved himself.

 Then Atreus, the godless father of this man,

 With more zeal than affection, pretended to arrange

 A day for the carving of meat as a welcome for my father,

 But the feast he provided was child-flesh.   1565

 He lopped off their feet and their fingers,

 Out of sight of the men who were sitting apart.

 Thyestes in his ignorance took the meat at once

 And ate it – food that would extinguish his line, you understand.

 And then, when he realised the terrible thing he had done,   1570

 He cried out; he falls back and vomits up that butchery,

 And as he prayed that Pelops' house suffer unbearable ruin,

 He kicks the banquet over, to match his curse

 That the whole race of Pleisthenes perish in the same way.

 Now you can see why this man fell;   1575

 And it was just that I be the one to tailor his murder.

 I was the third child and he drove me, with my poor father,

 Into exile, a little thing in swaddling-clothes,

 But Justice brought me back, a full-grown man.

Aegisthus' role in the murder

1581 I put together the whole grim plan   Aegisthus expresses personal satisfaction (1553) at Agamemnon's murder. Clytaemnestra boasted that the killing was her doing (1376) as Cassandra had foretold (1201). Now Aegisthus says he planned it (1576, 1581). To him it is payment (1549) for Atreus' crimes against Thyestes (1554) rather than revenge for Iphigeneia's death. Aegisthus avoids mention of Thyestes' adultery, to which Cassandra has referred (1164), seeing the feud of his father and uncle as a power struggle (1558). He does not mention Clytaemnestra: this is not a crime of love but revenge.
- How do you react to Aegisthus' account of his role in the murder?

1588 stones   See note on 1089.

1589 though you sit below at the oars   In Aegisthus' metaphor the Chorus play no part in the running of the 'ship' (Argos); he and Clytaemnestra control it from the 'helmsman's bench' (throne).
- What does this image reveal about Aegisthus' attitudes?
- How has his manner changed since he learnt of the Chorus' hostility (1587–8)?

Male and female

1597 you woman   The woman (Clytaemnestra) has increasingly shown the qualities of man (see **Male and female** pages 2, 30 and 48); she has also usurped Aegisthus' role in the traditional story (see *Background to the story*). In the Chorus' eyes, Aegisthus is now the woman (see note on 1408).

1601 Orpheus   is a poet and singer in mythology. He can sing so well that animals and even trees are charmed by his music and follow him.

Aegisthus as new king

1605 you will be king   Clytaemnestra called Aegisthus her shield, who gave her courage (1410). She has ceded to him Agamemnon's position as husband and king, and Agamemnon's wealth (1611). The Chorus call him a woman (1597) and intimate that he is a coward (1606, 1616, 1637).
- What impression does he create as he argues with the Chorus?
- What sort of ruler is he likely to be?

1612 no well-fed trace-horse   The trace-horse (see note on 816) receives special food because of his special role.

1618 Orestes sees the light of day somewhere   The Chorus see but one hope: they know that Orestes has an obligation to avenge his father (see **Agamemnon's avenger** page 96) and they hope that the *daimōn* (see *Daimōn* page 58) of the house will oversee his return to discharge it (1639).

Far away though I was, I laid hands on this man   1580
As I put together the whole grim plan.
So it is that even death would be sweet,
Now I have seen him in the nets of Justice.

CHORUS Aegisthus, I loathe the man who is arrogant in his crimes.
You declare that you willingly murdered this man,   1585
And planned this deplorable murder on your own;
I declare that you will not escape the curses on your head,
The stones which our people will throw as justice is done.

AEGISTHUS Is that what you say, though you sit below at the oars
And the ship's masters are up on the helmsman's bench?   1590
You are an old man, and you will learn how hard it is
For one your age to be taught a lesson, after being warned
To see sense. But manacles and hunger-pains are excellent,
Inspired healers of the mind and school even old age.
You can see, but not see this? Do not kick   1595
Against the pricks, lest you are hurt by your own blows.

CHORUS So, you woman, you waited for those
Who returned from battle, staying at home and all the while
Shaming a husband's bed, as you plotted the death of our general?

AEGISTHUS These words too will be parents to a family of screams;   1600
Orpheus had a tongue the opposite of yours:
He captivated all things in their delight at his voice,
But you will be led off into captivity because your senseless barking
Is so infuriating; submission will make you more docile.

CHORUS So you will be king of us Argives,   1605
You who did not dare, after you had plotted his death,
To do the actual deed and kill him yourself.

AEGISTHUS Deception was clearly a role for his wife:
I was his enemy and long viewed with suspicion.
Now, I will make every effort to rule the citizens   1610
Using his wealth; and I shall place a heavy yoke on the man
Who will not obey me, he will be no well-fed trace-horse.
Residing in darkness and grim starvation
Shall see him softened up.

Confrontation

1622 our work is at hand   The Chorus, old, unwarlike (78) and armed only with sticks (75), are provoked to combat (1622) against Aegisthus' guards (1623). Aegisthus is eager to assert his authority (1611–14) but before there is any fighting (see **Violence offstage** page 100), Clytaemnestra intervenes to defuse the situation (1626). The Chorus remain defiant to the end.

● Has your opinion of the Chorus changed during the course of the play?

1632 talons of the *daimōn*   The *daimōn* that is attacking the house (see ***Daimōn*** page 58; lines 1441, 1541) is now likened to a bird of prey.

Final impression of Clytaemnestra

1633 a woman's reasoning   Clytaemnestra makes one final pointed remark about women (334, 1372), and with her last words (1645) reminds the Chorus that she and Aegisthus share authority (see **Authority** page 26).

● Is Clytaemnestra in any way subservient?
○ It is rare for a tragedy not to end with a brief ode, sung by the Chorus prior to their leaving the stage. How do the Chorus leave the stage?
○ How do Aegisthus and Clytaemnestra leave? Is there a clue in 1643?
○ What is the most important final impression to convey?

The story continues

Choephoroi (*Libation Bearers*): Orestes returns to Argos and pays his respects at his father's tomb. His sister Electra arrives with the Chorus of female slaves (the libation bearers); they mourn their dead father together. He explains that Apollo's oracle has ordered him to avenge his father, threatening him with being hounded by Furies if he fails to do so. He goes to the palace in disguise, pretending he has news that Orestes is dead; Clytaemnestra welcomes him and sends for Aegisthus. Orestes kills him, then reveals his identity to Clytaemnestra, who asks for mercy. He refuses and leads her inside the palace. After killing her, he starts to see Furies hounding him for his matricide; he leaves for Delphi, to seek purification from Apollo.

Eumenides (*Kindly Ones*): Apollo's priestess at Delphi explains that she can see the Furies surrounding Orestes as he seeks purification at Apollo's shrine. Apollo promises to protect Orestes and summons Hermes to escort him to Athens for judgement. Clytaemnestra's ghost appears and urges the Furies to pursue him to Athens. In Athens a trial is arranged, with Orestes in the dock, Apollo for the defence and the Furies for the prosecution; the judges are ordinary citizens. After both sides have put their case the jury cast their votes. Athena then adds her decisive vote, and Orestes is acquitted. The Furies are outraged and threaten Athens with disaster, but Athena works to placate them with promises of privileges and honours. The Furies are appeased (becoming the Kindly Ones) and promise to protect Athens.

CHORUS Vicious by nature, why did you not kill   1615
This man yourself rather than use a woman,
A stain on our country and native gods,
To kill him? Oh that Orestes sees the light of day somewhere,
So he may return here by the grace of fortune
And become the all-conquering killer of them both.   1620

AEGISTHUS If you mean to behave like this, you will soon learn.

CHORUS Well then, friends and comrades, our work is at hand.

AEGISTHUS Well then, everyone, hands on your swords, ready!

CHORUS I stand at the ready too and am not afraid to die.

AEGISTHUS We welcome your talk of dying and accept the risk.   1625

CLYTAEMNESTRA My darling, let us not do further harm,
These events are already a miserable harvest, too much to reap.
There has been enough suffering: let us not shed blood. Old men,
Go to your rightful homes, before you suffer for your actions:
What we have done was right and necessary.   1630
We would settle for this, if it meant the end of our troubles,
So badly have we been crushed in the strong talons of the *daimōn*.
This is a woman's reasoning – should anyone think it worth knowing.

AEGISTHUS That these men pick me the fruit of their foolish tongues,
Trying their luck by throwing out comments like that!   1635
That they should fail to see sense and challenge their ruler!

CHORUS It is not the Argive way, to fawn on a coward.

AEGISTHUS I will still be after you in the days to come.

CHORUS Not if the *daimōn* guides Orestes to return.

AEGISTHUS I know that exiled men feed on hope.   1640

CHORUS Go on, grow fat defiling justice while you can.

AEGISTHUS Be sure I will make you pay for your stupidity.

CHORUS Yes, swagger and boast like some cock beside his hen.

CLYTAEMNESTRA Do not pay any heed to their futile snarling:
You and I have authority here, and we will put the house to rights. 1645

Synopsis of the play

PROLOGUE (1–39)

King Agamemnon has been absent from Argos for ten years, leading the Greek expedition against Troy. Every night a watchman has lain awake at his post at the palace in Argos, watching for the fire-signal that Troy has been captured. He suddenly sees the fire-signal giving him that news: he is ecstatic and quickly passes the message to Clytaemnestra, the queen.

PARODOS (40–243)

The Chorus of old men of Argos enter. They sing of the background to the Trojan War: the abduction of Helen, the departure of the expedition to rescue her, the omen and delay at Aulis, the sacrifice of Iphigeneia. They finish with a request to Clytaemnestra to explain how she can be so sure Troy has been sacked.

FIRST EPISODE (244–340)

Clytaemnestra explains that she had organised a relay of fire-signals all the way from Troy to Argos, so that she could learn of Troy's capture almost as soon as it happened. She then pictures the scene in Troy after its capture.

FIRST STASIMON (341–469)

The Chorus respond to this news with a celebration: Zeus has ensured that Paris and Troy have been punished for the abduction of Helen. They recall that abduction, its effect on Menelaus and its consequences for the people of Greece, who began to resent the war, its cause and its cost. Thus the atmosphere of celebration at the beginning of the stasimon has turned into one of fear and gloom by its end.

SECOND EPISODE (470–661)

A herald arrives from Troy, relieved to be back home alive. He stresses the justice of the Greek cause to regain Helen and then gives details of the struggle at Troy. Clytaemnestra expresses her joy at this confirmation that Troy has been captured. In response to an enquiry from the Chorus, the herald then recounts the storm on the journey home that separated Menelaus from Agamemnon and the rest of the fleet.

SECOND STASIMON (662–756)

The Chorus sing of the consequences of Helen's abduction for the Trojans. They picture the arrival of Helen at Troy and then reflect on its repercussions. As they recall Paris' abduction of Helen, they are led to consider why it is that men commit wicked and arrogant acts.

THIRD EPISODE (757–947)

Agamemnon returns triumphant to Argos, having sacked Troy; he is accompanied by Cassandra, the prize given him by the army. The Chorus welcome him, but try to convey a warning not to trust everyone. He greets his native land and its gods and addresses the Chorus. Clytaemnestra then explains how difficult it was for her while Agamemnon was absent. She arranges for an expensive cloth to be laid out for him to walk on into the palace; at first he is reluctant, but she persuades him to walk on it, and he goes inside.

THIRD *STASIMON* (948–1004)

The Chorus express a sense of foreboding. Although it has been a long time since the expedition left Aulis and though they have witnessed Agamemnon's safe return home themselves, they are still concerned. They do not explain exactly what they fear.

FOURTH EPISODE (1005–1301)

Clytaemnestra summons Cassandra into the palace. The latter gives no indication that she hears or understands anything Clytaemnestra says, but starts to go into the state of trance preliminary to receiving a vision. Clytaemnestra becomes impatient and goes back inside the palace. Cassandra then undergoes a series of visions: she sees the butchery of Thyestes' children, then Agamemnon's murder and finally her own imminent death. Because the Chorus are unable to follow her meaning, she describes her visions a second time in simpler language, but the Chorus still do not grasp her meaning fully. After a few final thoughts and predictions, she goes inside the palace.

FOURTH *STASIMON* (1302–13)

The Chorus start to sing about success and its transient nature, but Agamemnon's death cries cut the *stasimon* off abruptly.

FIFTH EPISODE (1314–1548)

Clytaemnestra emerges from the palace with the bodies of Agamemnon and Cassandra. She explains how she lied in order to put Agamemnon at his ease, and relives his murder in graphic detail. The Chorus are horrified, but Clytaemnestra continues to justify the murders, mainly citing the sacrifice of Iphigeneia. The Chorus mourn the dead Agamemnon, but Clytaemnestra counters each stanza of lament with one criticising the dead Agamemnon or exulting in his death.

EXODOS (1549–1645)

Aegisthus enters. He explains the reasons for his satisfaction at Agamemnon's death, which he sees as just revenge for the death of Thyestes' children. The Chorus reproach him and he responds with threats: they almost come to blows, but Clytaemnestra intervenes. Aegisthus and Clytaemnestra then leave and the play ends.

Pronunciation of names

To attempt the authentic pronunciation of Classical Greek names presents great difficulties. It is perhaps easiest to accept the conventional anglicised versions of the familiar names (e.g. Ares, Zeus). The key below offers help with all the names in the play, which will give a reasonable overall consistency. Note that the main stress occurs on the italicised syllable.

> **KEY**
>
> *ay* – as in 'hay'   *ch* – as in Scottish 'loch'
> *ē* – as in 'hair'   *ī* – as in 'die'
> *ō* – long 'o', as in 'go'

Achaea	A-*chee*-a	Geryon	*Ge*-ri-ōn
Acheron	A-che-rōn	Gorgopis	Gorg-*ōp*-is
Aegean	Ee-*jee*-an	Hades	*Hay*-dees
Aegisthus	Ee-*gis*-thus	Helios	*Hee*-li-os
Agamemnon	A-ga-*mem*-nōn	Hellas	*Hel*-las
Amphisbaina	Am-fis-*bī*-na	Hephaestus	He-*fis*-tus
Aphrodite	A-fro-*dī*-tē	Heracles	*Hē*-rak-lēs
Apollo	A-*pol*-lō	Hermes	*Her*-mees
Arachnaeon	A-rach-*nī*-on	Ida	*Ī*-da
Ares	*Air*-reez	Ilian	*Ī*-li-an
Artemis	*Ar*-te-mis	Ilium	*Ī*-li-um
Asopus	A-*sō*-pus	Iphigeneia	I-fi-gen-*ay*-a
Athos	*A*-thos	Itys	*Ī*-tis
Atreidae	A-*tre*-i-dī	Leda	*Lee*-da
Atreides	A-*tre*-i-dees	Lemnos	*Lem*-nos
Atreus	*Ay*-tre-us	Loxias	*Lo*-xi-as
Aulis	*Ow*-lis	Lyceian	*Lī*-see-an
Calchas	*Kal*-kas	Makistos	Ma-*kis*-tos
Cassandra	Kas-*san*-dra	Menelaus	Me-ne-*lay*-us
Chalcis	*Kal*-kis	Messapion	Mes-*sa*-pi-on
Chryses	*Chrī*-sees	Odysseus	O-*dis*-se-us
Cithaeron	Ki-*thī*-rōn	Orestes	O-*res*-tees
Clytaemnestra	Klī-tem-*nes*-tra	Orpheus	*Or*-fe-us
Cocytus	Kō-*sī*-tus	Pelops	*Pe*-lops
Danaan	Da-*nay*-an	Phocian	Fō-*see*-an
Erinyes	E-*rī*-ni-es	Phocis	*Fō*-sis
Erinys	E-*rī*-nis	Pleiades	*Plī*-a-dees
Euripus	Eu-*rī*-pus	Pleisthenes	*Plī*-sthe-nees

Priam	*Pri*-am	Teucer	*Tyoo*-ser
Saronic	Sa-*ro*-nic	Thrace	Thrays
Scamander	Ska-*man*-der	Thracian	*Thray*-si-an
Scylla	*Sil*-la	Thyestes	Thī-*es*-tees
Simois	*Si*-mō-is	Trojan	*Trō*-jan
Strophius	*Strō*-fi-us	Tyndareus	Tin-*da*-re-us
Strymon	*Stri*-mōn	Zephyr	*Ze*-fer
Tantalus	*Tan*-ta-lus	Zeus	Zyoos

Introduction to the Greek Theatre

Theātron, the Greek word that gave us 'theatre' in English, meant both 'viewing place' and the assembled viewers. These ancient viewers (*theātai*) were in some ways very different from their modern counterparts. For a start, they were participants in a religious festival, and they went to watch plays only on certain days in the year, when shows were put on in honour of Dionysus. At Athens, where drama developed many of its most significant traditions, the main Dionysus festival, held in the spring, was one of the most important events in the city's calendar, attracting large numbers of citizens and visitors from elsewhere in the Greek world. It is not known for certain whether women attended; if any did, they were more likely to be visitors than the wives of Athenian citizens.

The festival was also a great sporting occasion. Performances designed to win the god's favour needed spectators to witness and share in the event, just as the athletic contests did at Olympia or Delphi, and one of the ways in which the spectators got involved was through competition. What they saw were three sets of three tragedies plus a satyr-play, five separate comedies and as many as twenty song-and-dance performances called dithyrambs, put on in honour of Dionysus by choruses representing the different 'tribes' into which the citizen body was divided. There was a contest for each different event, with the dithyramb choruses divided into men's and boys' competitions, and a panel of judges determined the winners. The judges were appointed to act on behalf of the city; no doubt they took some notice of the way the audience responded on each occasion. Attendance at these events was on a large scale: we should be thinking of football crowds rather than typical theatre audiences in the modern world.

Like football matches, dramatic festivals were open-air occasions, and the performances were put on in daylight rather than with stage lighting in a darkened auditorium. The ideal performance space in these circumstances was a hollow hillside to seat spectators, with a flat area at the bottom (*orchēstra*) in which the chorusmen could spread out for their dancing and singing and which could be closed off by a stage-building (*skēnē*) acting simultaneously as backdrop, changing room and sounding board. Effective acoustics and good sight-lines were achieved by the kind of design represented in Fig. A on page 127, the theatre of Dionysus at Athens. The famous stone theatre at Epidaurus (Fig. B), built about 330 BC, and often taken as typical, has a circular *orchēstra*, but in the fifth century it was normal practice for theatres to have a low wooden stage in front of the *skēnē*, for use by

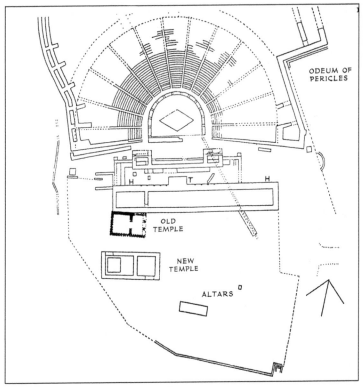

Fig. A. The theatre of Dionysus at Athens.

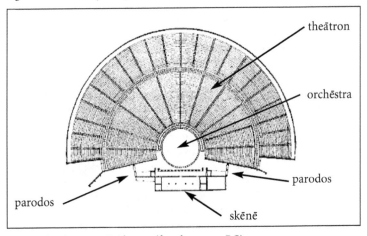

Fig. B. The theatre at Epidaurus (fourth century BC).

the actors, who also interacted with the chorus in the *orchēstra*.

Song and dance by choruses and the accompanying music of the piper were integral to all these types of performance and not just to the dithyramb. In tragedy there were 12 (later 15) chorusmen, in comedy 24, and in dithyramb 50; plays were often named after their chorus: Aeschylus' *Persians*, Euripides' *Bacchae* and Aristophanes' *Birds* are familiar examples. The rhythmic movements, groupings and singing of the chorus contributed crucially to the overall impact of each show, ensuring that there was always an animated stage picture even when only one or two actors were in view. The practice of keeping the number of speaking actors normally restricted to three, with doubling of roles by the same actor where necessary, looks odd at first sight, but it makes sense in the special circumstance of Greek theatrical performance. Two factors are particularly relevant: first the use of masks, which was probably felt to be fundamental to shows associated with the cult of Dionysus and which made it easy for an actor to take more than one part within a single play, and second the need to concentrate the audience's attention by keeping the number of possible speakers limited. In a large, open acting area some kind of focusing device is important if the spectators are always to be sure where to direct their gaze. The Greek plays that have survived, particularly the tragedies, are extremely economical in their design, with no sub-plots or complications in the action which audiences might find distracting or confusing. Acting style, too, seems to have relied on large gestures and avoidance of fussy detail; we know from the size of some of the surviving theatres that many spectators would be sitting too far away to catch small-scale gestures or stage business. Some plays make powerful use of props, like Ajax's sword, Philoctetes' bow, or the head of Pentheus in *Bacchae*, but all these are carefully chosen to be easily seen and interpreted.

Above all, actors seem to have depended on their highly trained voices in order to captivate audiences and stir their emotions. By the middle of the fifth century there was a prize for the best actor in the tragic competition, as well as for the playwright and the financial sponsor of the performance (*chorēgos*), and comedy followed suit a little later. What was most admired in the leading actors who were entitled to compete for this prize was the ability to play a series of different and very demanding parts in a single day and to be a brilliant singer as well as a compelling speaker of verse: many of the main parts involve solo songs or complex exchanges between actor and chorus. Overall, the best plays and performances must have offered audiences a great charge of energy and excitement: the chance to see a group of chorusmen dancing and singing in a sequence of different guises, as young maidens, old counsellors, ecstatic maenads, and exuberant satyrs; to watch scenes in which supernatural beings – gods, Furies, ghosts – come into contact with human beings; to listen to intense debates and hear the blood-curdling offstage cries that heralded the arrival of a messenger with an account of terrifying deeds within, and then to see the bodies brought out and witness the lamentations. Far more 'happened' in most plays than we can easily imagine from the bare text on the page; this must help to account for the continuing appeal of drama throughout antiquity and across the Greco-Roman world.

From the fourth century onwards dramatic festivals became popular wherever there were communities of Greek speakers, and other gods besides Dionysus were honoured with performances of plays. Actors, dancers and musicians organised themselves for professional touring – some of them achieved star status and earned huge fees – and famous old plays were revived as part of the repertoire. Some of the plays that had been first performed for Athenian citizens in the fifth century became classics for very different audiences – women as well as men, Latin speakers as well as Greeks – and took on new kinds of meaning in their new environment. But theatre was very far from being an antiquarian institution: new plays, new dramatic forms like mime and pantomime, changes in theatre design, staging, masks and costumes all demonstrate its continuing vitality in the Hellenistic and Roman periods. Nearly all the Greek plays that have survived into modern times are ones that had a long theatrical life in antiquity; this perhaps helps to explain why modern actors, directors and audiences have been able to rediscover their power.

For further reading: entries in *Oxford Classical Dictionary* (3rd edition) under 'theatre staging, Greek' and 'tragedy, Greek'; J.R. Green, 'The theatre', Ch. 7 of *The Cambridge Ancient History, Plates to Volumes V and VI*, Cambridge, 1994; Richard Green and Eric Handley, *Images of the Greek Theatre*, London, 1995; Rush Rehm, *Greek Tragic Theatre*, London and New York, 1992; P.E. Easterling (ed.), *The Cambridge Companion to Greek Tragedy*, Cambridge, 1997; David Wiles, *Tragedy in Athens*, Cambridge, 1997.

Pat Easterling

Time line

Dates of selected authors and extant works

12th century BC	The Trojan War	
8th century BC	HOMER	• *The Iliad* • *The Odyssey*
5th century BC 490–479 431–404	**The Persian wars** **The Peloponnesian wars**	

c. 525/4–456/5
 	
472
 	
456
	AESCHYLUS	(In probable order.)
		
		• *Persians*
		• *Seven against Thebes*
		• *Suppliants*
		• **Oresteia Trilogy:**
		  Agamemnon, Choephoroi
		  Eumenides
		• *Prometheus Bound*

c. 496/5–406 409 401 (posthumous)	SOPHOCLES	(Undated plays are in alphabetical order.) • *Ajax* • *Oedipus Tyrannus* • *Antigone* • *Trachiniae* • *Electra* • *Philoctetes* • *Oedipus at Colonus*
c. 490/80–407/6 438 (1st production 455) 431 428 415 412 409 ?408 ?408–6	EURIPIDES	(In probable order.) • *Alcestis* • *Medea* • *Heracleidae* • *Hippolytus* • *Andromache* • *Hecuba* • *Suppliant Women* • *Electra* • *Trojan Women* • *Heracles* • *Iphigenia among the Taurians* • *Helen* • *Ion* • *Phoenissae* • *Orestes* • *Cyclops* (satyr-play) • *Bacchae* • *Iphigenia at Aulis*
460/50–*c.* 386 411 405	ARISTOPHANES	(Selected works.) • *Thesmophoriazusae* • *Lysistrata* • *Frogs*
4th century BC 384–322	ARISTOTLE	(Selected works.) • *The Art of Poetry*

Index

Bold numbers refer to pages. Other numbers are line references.

CPSIA information can be obtained
at www.ICGtesting.com
Printed in the USA
LVHW021917270119
605446LV00011B/44/P